Mary E. Garber
419 Stratford
Winston. Salem
N.C.
1936

From Bed
to Worse

From Bed to Worse

OR COMFORTING THOUGHTS
ABOUT THE BISON

by
ROBERT BENCHLEY

Publishers
Harper & Brothers
New York and London
1934

Table
of Contents

vi

*From Bed
to Worse*

J'Accuse

LET'S have an end of all this shilly-shallying. *I* killed Rasputin. The thing has dragged on long enough, with even Mike Romanoff claiming that he did it, and my uncle claiming that it was done by the boys of his curling-club. Well, as a matter of fact, I am the one who did it, and here is how it happened.

We were sitting around in the cellar of the Winter Palace, Rasputin, Mike Romanoff, a Grand Duke whose name I have forgotten, and I. We had a couple of dancing bears in for the occasion, and things were beginning to get a little rowdy.

According to a pre-arranged plan between Mike Romanoff and myself, a tray of *hors d'oeuvres* was brought in for us to dip in our vodka. Each canape consisted of a little mound of elk-poison, covered with grated egg, and to make things safer, the egg had been poisoned, too. Four elk had been killed in the out-of-town try out, so Mike and I were in high good humor.

Naturally, the tray was passed first to Ras-

1

putin, for, if anyone else was served first, he was one mad monk, I can tell you. He took four canapes in one hand and two in the other, and put them all in his mouth at once. I took one and palmed it, and Mike said: "No, thanks. They're so much poison to me," which I thought was a pretty funny crack, coming from Mike. By this time, all eyes were on Rasputin.

He wiped the crumbs from his beard, took a swig of vodka, and said: "Those are mighty nice cookies. Where did you get them?" Then he got up and went to the window and looked out. "It looks like snow," he said. "By George, it *is* snow!" And he danced up and down in delight to see the little flakes swirling down through the air. Those Russians are just like kids when it starts to snow.

I looked at Mike and he shrugged his shoulders. "Mike," I said, "how about whamming old Rasputin over the head with that iron bell-clapper, just to see if he likes butter?"

Rasputin turned to see what was up, just as Mike crashed down on him with the heavy clapper we had taken from the church of St. Sophia earlier that day. The hair on the Mad Monk's head went down so far that it got into the hair of his beard, but he opened up a little space in it with his fingers, and said:

2

"Come on, cut out this kidding! I've got work to do this afternoon, even if you boys haven't."

"You try it, Bob," said Mike, trying to dislodge the clapper. So I took out my gun, and holding Rasputin at arm's length, said: "One to get ready—two to start—and three to go—o!" I fired four times into him, and hit him over the head with the gun-butt for the pay-off. I have never seen a guy so sore in my life.

"Hey, what is this?" he said. "Let somebody else be It for a while. I'm all out of breath." So I made believe that we were friends again, and put my arm around his shoulder.

"O. K., Rasputin," I said, "let byegones be byegones, and don't be a baby all your life. What about a little stroll down to the lake to throw fire-crackers at the fish?"

He was pleased as Punch at the idea, and we walked arm in arm, down to the lake, which was frozen over, except around the edges. Rasputin tried to hypnotize me on the way, but I slapped him down. "None of your mad monk-ey business," I said, and, while he was laughing at my play on words, I rolled him under the edge of the ice so far, that I had to put skates on to get out to where he was.

I skated around him for a while, cutting

figure eights, until Mike joined me, and then we two went fishing through the ice for him. Every time we caught him, we threw him back, until finally, tiring of our sport, we replaced the block of ice over the hole, stamped it down and left him.

Now that is the true story of how Rasputin was killed, and I don't think there's a jury in the country that would convict me. So let's have no more talk about it, please.

This Week's Horoscope

WE ENTER this week into the influence of a recently discovered planet which has completely disrupted the science of astrology: that of Avis (the Bird). All those who were born during this week, or in any week in good aspect with any of the other planets, and all those attempting any financial, amatory, or even ambulatory enterprises, will be distinctly out of luck. Staying indoors, preferably in a closet, is indicated until we are out of the orbit of Avis. Coming out of the closet after that is optional, but not recommended.

Avis was originally supposed to govern the destinies only of horse-racing, filling inside-straights, and playing quarter gambling machines in saloons, but during the past three years it has extended its influence until it embraces practically every form of human activity, except possibly stacking the dishes until morning and not shaving. It is favorable to procrastinators and people who sleep a lot, for, under it, those who don't do anything at all

have the satisfaction of not having done anything wrong. All others spend the following
weeks kicking themselves.

Let us take up the specific days of the week
and see what is in store for us:

SATURDAY, August 13—In the early morning
those having an inclination to get out of bed
will not find things going their way. Left shoes
will be hard to find, shaving water will not run
hot, and four-minute eggs will be found to have
been boiled two minutes. If possible, it will be
better to remain in bed until noon, being careful not to lie too close to the edge. A sharp eye
should also be kept on the plaster above the
bed. Later in the day things will be a little
better, as the chances of making unwise investments will have been decreased by one-half.
Perhaps a little turn around the room with the
aid of a stick will do no harm, although the
stick should not be too sharp and should under
no circumstances be swung off the ground. A
little clear soup may be eaten, very slowly to
avoid choking.

SUNDAY, August 14—This will be a good day,
in comparison with the rest of the week, for
there will not be so many trucks in the streets
and people stay indoors more anyway. If in the
country, all invitations to play tennis, go swimming or paddling, or even to take long walks

in the hills, should be sternly refused. (This will be a good out for a great many people who don't want to indulge in these exercises anyway. Don't forget to take this horoscope along with you to show your host as proof.) For those who like to play games of chance *for fun*, the late afternoon and early evening will be propitious. Any seafood which has been kept in the house since Saturday should be avoided.

A child born on this day will have better luck than its father, but will inherit a tendency to unwise investments.

MONDAY, August 15—Let's not talk about this day.

TUESDAY, August 16—Profit (intellectual) and pleasure will accrue to those who visit free museums and picture galleries today, while places of historical interest, if they are not situated under overhanging cliffs or in too-ramshackle structures, can't do a bit of harm. In the way of financial ventures, a good government bond may be bought without too much risk. (Mind, we said "a good government.")

WEDNESDAY, August 17—This will be a day of petty annoyances and trifling worries—in other words, a comparatively good day. People sailing on ships will be especially irritated with passport troubles and insufficiency of passage money. People landing on ships will have to

7

sneak off without tipping the last two stewards on their lists. Those giving parties will run out of vermouth and have to shift to orange juice. But the larger disappointments and failures will be held in abeyance today. Saving up for tomorrow.

THURSDAY, August 18—A honey. Mark this off on your calendar and pull the blinds down. Today's child would do well to reconsider the whole thing and ask to be scratched. If you thought that Monday was bad, just poke your head outdoors along about six P.M. today and look around. The day will be propitious, however, for high-class murdering and arson, provided you take care not to burn yourself in the latter venture.

FRIDAY, August 19—Along about noon of today, we emerge from the influence of Avis, but nobody should take it seriously until about three P.M., after the Stock Exchange has closed. Then go very cautiously, gradually working up a mild elation along about ten P.M. After that it will be all right to slap someone on the back, provided he isn't averse to being slapped on the back under the best of conditions. Things will go a little better from now on, but don't make a fool of yourself just because you have been tipped off. We merely said "better."

8

A Brief Study
of Dendrophilism

DENDROPHILISM (love of trees) is of comparatively recent origin as a study in *psychopathia sexualis,* owing to the comparatively recent discovery of trees. It is really quite a thing.

The manifestations of dendrophilism are: (1) the patient gets a crush on certain trees, or even trees in general, often resulting in futile attempts at flirting and necking; (2) there is, after a preliminary period of promiscuity, a desire to marry some good tree and settle down; (3) extreme embarrassment occurs when in the presence of trees, expressed by blushing and tripping over small objects on the ground. There is also, in some cases, an irresistible desire to steal trees and take them home. This, except in the case of saplings, is so impractical as to cause the patient considerable nervousness and a constant sense of bafflement.

The history of dendrophilism (from the Greek *dendron,* meaning "tree," and *ophilism,* meaning "fun with") leads us into the high-

9

ways and byways of pathology. Charcot and Magnan, in 1882, in the *"Archives de Neurologie at Souvenirs d'un Voyage en Orient,"* first mention it as a phenomenon among the Dorian Greeks (see "Dorian Gray"), although in the *"Jahrbuch für Sexuelle Zwischenstufen"* (Ginn & Co., 1880) we find it referred to as a form of botany.

It was not, however, until Näcke, in 1906, found it prevalent among the Alaska Eskimos, complicated to a serious degree by the lack of trees in Alaska, that it was recognized as a form of something of importance to the social order. Up until then it was just thought that certain people were crazy about trees, that was all.

Baumann, in his *"Zeitschrift für Ethnologie und Bilderbuch für Kinder"* (1891) does refer to a custom among the Negro population of New Guinea of dressing trees up in costumes and taking them out to parties, but nobody thought anything of it at the time. More recently, Sainte-Claire Deville ("Five Little Peppers Grown Up," 1899) observed that certain older members of Albanian tribes, if kept away from starchy foods too long, show a marked tendency to hang around the branches of the more attractive trees in the neighborhood, thereby causing quite a lot of talk and rather making fools of themselves.

This, too, has been noted by Bethe in his *"Rhenisches museum für Philologie,"* although he had an idea that this behavior was due merely to nervousness and a lack of interest in going home. He was under the impression that oaktrees were the only trees used in this connection, and therefore referred to the phenomenon as *Eichesucht* (lust for oaks), not to be confused with the word *Eifersucht* (jealousy), although there is a case on record in Langsdorff's "Voyages and Travels in Sun-Lit Seas" in which a *burdash* among the Tahiti Indians once killed a rival who had usurped his rights in a cypress. It is therefore possible that the word *Eichesucht* derives from *Eifersucht,* but this is not considered likely, even by people who consider *any*thing likely.

There is a custom among the northern tribes of Unyamweizi and Uganda of getting all the young trees together once a year and trimming them with ropes of teeth, after which a festival of sometimes the wildest nature is indulged in. The elders of the tribe dance about the trees in a pretty silly fashion and fall down continuously, giving the impression that they are simply mad about one tree or another. It ends up in nothing at all happening.

In America, dendrophilism has not gained much headway, owing to there being so many other things to take up people's minds, although Kiernan, in the Detroit *Lancet,* does mention a case of a woman in Grand Rapids who was under suspicion of going pretty strongly for an old elm, which she claimed had been in the family for a hundred years and which she wanted to have brought into the house just to keep her company. Her relatives, however, persuaded her against this, on account of the possibility of falling leaves cluttering up the living-room.

Among the concomitant phenomena of dendrophilism are: (1) hiding in hollow oaks, (2) carving initials in the bark of trees, (3) sleeping in branches, (4) pressing autumn leaves in books, (5) running head-on into large trees on bicycles.

The lines of treatment when dendrophilism exists are the following (if any one cares enough to try) :

1. Cutting down all trees in the neighborhood.

2. Cure of the neurosis by means of hypnotic suggestion, the patient being made to say a

hundred times before going to bed each night: "I don't give a darn if I never see another tree."

3. Foot baths (24° to 20° R.) ; extr. Secal. cornut. aquos., 0.5; anti-pyrin, 1.0 (*pro die*) ; pot. brom. 4.0 (evenings) .

4. Cultivation of outside interests, such as good books, skating, heavy drinking, and tall, willowy, blonde girls.

Suggested collateral reading: "The Menace of the Tree," by Ludwig Lascha; "Unattractive Trees: Their Prevention and Cure," by Dr. Asa Altemus; "Trees—Ugh!," an anthology of anti-tree poetry; "The Great Horse-Chestnut Blight of 1907," Am. Journal of Tree Surgery, 1910.

CASES

(In the following histories we must make allowances for the natural exaggeration in psychopathic cases, especially among dendrophilists, who, it will be understood, must have rather strong imaginations.)

HISTORY I. Mr. R. S., aged 31, German of French descent. Paternal ancestors normal, so far as he knows. He is fair, slight, and refined in appearance, except for very tight colored collars, which he wears with ties which do not match his shirt. Indifferent to exercise and sports. Favorite color, green. Given to romping when drunk. Can whistle.

"When I was a child," he writes, "I was of an affec-

13

tionate disposition, but not enough to get arrested. I have always been attracted to trees, especially poplars. At the age of 8, I climbed a poplar and was brought down only by a pack of beagles, who made life in the tree miserable for me *eodem tempore aliquam diu ab initio fui.*

"At the age of 12, I was sent away to boarding school, where I made the acquaintance of several boys who were keen on gathering chestnuts, and we used to go out into the woods and scrape around among the leaves until we found the objects of our craving. I was not aware at the time of the significance of this act.

"On going to the University, I became definitely addicted to tree-climbing, but, as there were few trees in the neighborhood, I became inhibited and jumpy. It was not until I took a course in forestry that I was able to indulge my hobby, and have, ever since then, been found in whatever arboretum the locality may boast, breaking off branches and running home with them. My married life is very happy and I have a whole attic full of branches which I have arranged alphabetically."

HISTORY II. Mr. X., aged 49; Vienna; married since 1900. Always sullen and silent. Father neuropathic but awfully good company on a party. X. has long been troubled with alternation of causeless depression, with *tædium vitæ*, and periods of elation. During the latter climbs trees constantly, calling out to people below: "Look at me, where *I* am!" Doesn't care whether he is cured or not, and if he doesn't, who does?

Other case in APPENDIX D.

14

Saturday's Smells

NEVER, even in my best form, what you would call a "drone" or "worker" at heart, I have been having a particularly tough time of it lately just sitting at my desk.

Specialists and psychoanalysts from all over the world have been working on my case, and it was only yesterday that I myself was able to give them the key to my inability to work. It is my new pipe tobacco. It smells like Saturday, and consequently puts me in a chronic holiday mood.

This may take a little explaining. The main thesis on which I am going to build my case is that, when you were a child, certain days had their individual smells, and that these smells, when experienced today, take you back to your state of mind when you experienced them in childhood. Do I make myself clear, or must I say that all over again?

Sunday smells were, of course, the most distinctive, and, when they assail me today, I become restless and depressed and want to go to sea. In my section of the country, the first Sunday smell was of the fish-balls for breakfast. This was not so depressing, as fish-balls were good, and anyway, Sunday didn't begin to get you down until later in the day.

Then came, in slow succession, the musty draughts of the Sunday-school vestry, laden with the week's dust on the maps of Palestine and the hymnals, and freshened that morning only by the smell of black silk dresses sprinkled with lavendar and the starch from little girls' petticoats and sashes. Then the return to the home, where fish-cakes had given way to fricasseeing chicken and boiling onions, which, in turn, gave way to the aroma of the paternal cigar as you started out on that Sunday afternoon walk, during which you passed all the familiar spots where you had been playing only the day before with the gang, now desolate and small-looking in the pall of Sunday.

But, sure as the smells of Sunday were, those of Saturday were none the less distinctive and a great deal more cheery. In our house we began getting whiffs of Saturday as early as Friday evening, when the bread was "set" on the kitchen table and the beans "put to soak" nearby. The smell of the cold bread-dough when the napkins were lifted from the pans

16

always meant "no school tomorrow," and was a preliminary to the "no school today" smells of Saturday, which are at the basis of my present trouble.

On Saturday morning early these "no school today" smells began to permeate the kitchen, and, as the kitchen was the sole port of entry and exit during the morning's play outside, they became inextricably mixed up with not only cooking, but "duck-on-the-rock," "Indian guide" and that informal scrimmaging which boys indulge in in back yards, which goes by the name of either "football" or "baseball" according to the season of the year.

In New England, of course, the *leit motif* among the Saturday smells was the one of beans baking, but the bread and pies ran it a close second. A good cake in the oven could hold its own, too. Then, along about eleven-thirty the Saturday noon dinner began to loom up, being more plebeian than the Sunday noon dinner, it usually took the combined form of cabbage, turnips, beets and corned beef, all working together in one pot, with the potatoes, to make what is known as the "New England boiled dinner." That put a stop to any other smells that thought they were something earlier in the morning.

17

On the outside, Saturday morning contributed the smell of burning leaves, and of shingles on the new house that was always being built in the neighborhood; and, although sounds do not come into our lecture today, there was the sound of carpenters hammering, and the re-echoing beat of rugs being dusted, which became almost smells in their affinity to them.

Now, here is the point about my pipe tobacco. A month or so ago I tried out a new blend, which, I discovered only yesterday, smells exactly like beans in an oven. So, when I settle down to a morning's work and light my pipe, I am gradually overcome with the delicious feeling that there is "no school today," and that I really ought to be outdoors playing.

So, without knowing why, I have been leaving my work and getting out my skates and yielding to the Saturday spirit. The only trouble has been that, under this subtle influence, every day has been Saturday, because every day has smelled like Saturday.

I don't suppose that the tradesmen to whom I owe money will think much of this explanation, but it satisfies me and the psychoanalysts perfectly. And, as yet, I have made no move to buy a less insidious-smelling pipe tobacco.

The Devil's Diamond

Is the famous Imky diamond a hoodoo? Is it a diamond? Is it Imky? These are three of the five questions that students of the occult are asking themselves. (The other two questions are: 1. What three famous generals never saw each other? 2. Where is Arithmetic?) That low buzz-buzz-buzz is the sound of students of the occult asking themselves questions. The following silence is their failure to reply.

FOR the riddle of the Imky diamond has been a source of puzzlement to scientists for the past fifty years. . . . Oh, well, forty-five then. . . . Thirty. . . . Twenty. . . . Six, and not a year less. That's final. Since it was first brought from India by Lieutenant Colonel Irving Imky, shortly after the Ski Rebellion, it has been passed from generation to generation of this unhappy family, always bringing death, famine, and similar bits of hard luck in its wake until the present members of the family have begun to wonder if perhaps it would not be better to get rid of it altogether. In fact, they *would* get rid of it—if they could find it. For in addition to its almost spooky quality of bearing misfortune to its owner, it has added insult to injury and got itself lost.

"It is somewhere about the house, I am sure," said Mrs. The Honorable Imky to a reporter yesterday, "for it is still giving off hard luck. That is the unfortunate part of the affair—we haven't the satisfaction of taking it out and looking at it, but it is being just as naughty as it was in the old days. If we could find it, we would throw it out and maybe get some sleep."

The first indication that the diamond was not a good-luck piece was when the old Lieutenant Colonel bought it from the Indian rajah and immediately fell down and broke both hips. He did not at first attribute the accident to the diamond, as he had been drinking rather heavily (otherwise he never would have bought it) and had been falling down constantly for two years. But this was the first time that he had suffered any injury more serious than slight abrasions and nose-bendings. They put him on a boat bound for England, he still clutching the jewel in his hand, as he would not trust it to his *punkah*. Shortly after leaving Singapore, the ship ran into a large rock (which later turned out to be the mainland) and the unlucky Imky's state-room, which was forward on the starboard side, was pushed aft and slightly to port so far that he ended up in the galley, in no very good frame of mind I can assure you. In fact, there was some doubt as to whether his stateroom was on the ship at all and, for a day or two, he was listed as "not having sailed." This little *contretemps* did his hips no good, either, and by the time he had landed in London he was far from the dapper young officer who had sailed ten years before to serve Her Majesty the Queen. But he still held the diamond clutched in his chubby fist and showed it to people with great pride, saying, "Look!"

During the rest of his life (about four days) he refused to relinquish his prize, and when he was buried in Westminster Abbey (he was a very large man and there was some talk of bury-ing Westminster Abbey in *him,* but this was given up because of the engineering difficulties in the way) another stone, of the same size and shape, had to be substituted for the real dia-mond, otherwise they never could have got him to lie down.

The gem then passed into the possession of his eldest son, Lord Inverness Imky, who was asleep at the time and didn't realize what he had inherited until the next day when the roof fell in. "What is this?" he asked, petulantly, from under a large glass chandelier. "Somebody wise-cracking?" When he was told that it was probably the work of the Imky diamond, which was then reposing in his strong box along with 3000 pounds' worth of bills which his father had bequeathed him, he merely nodded (as well as he could with the chandelier around his neck) and said: "We Imkys must play the game and carry on to see it through, and cheerie-ho!" Then he collapsed and was buried in Westminster Abbey, much to the surprise of Lord Alfred Tennyson.

The next of kin to catch hell was the younger brother of Lord Inverness, who, by now, was in so much trouble in his own right that he hardly noticed the effect of the diamond. When, one day shortly after he had come into his heritage, his right arm dropped off, he laid it to some boyhood prank and thought nothing of it. "I shall be all right," he said, pluckily. "I've seen everything, anyway." But he was *not* all right, and the diamond, evidently piqued at not being credited with this odd piece of misfortune, set itself to showing the young man what was what.

Hearing that there was a great future for left-handed men in America, the scion of this

22

ancient family migrated and settled in New York (in the State of New York). He did not take the diamond with him, as he left England rather hurriedly, owing to a little killing in which he had played quarterback, but he had not been in New York for more than a month before the precious stone followed him, working its way over on a cattleship under the name of Townsend. It showed up one day at his lodgings and that very evening New York was destroyed by the Great Chicago Fire. So much for superstition.

And so it has gone. The Imkys have prospered, in the material sense of the word (which is about as good a sense as you can get out of a word like "prospered"), having sold old Indians to New York for a string of beads and then flooded the market with new Indians. The Indians themselves enjoyed this little game of give and take and the Indian trade was brisk on Broadway for a good many years; so brisk indeed that additions had to be built to most of the speakeasies just to accommodate the Indian trade. Most of the drinking Indians were two-bottle men and always after the second bottle they would insist upon giving portions of Manhattan to their white friends. And it was precisely in this manner that the island of Man-

23

hattan and subsequently all of America came finally into the hands of the White Fathers. So the Imkys have established a business here which, while it sagged a little during the Depression of 1929-78, has brought them in thousands of inquiries and promises to pay. They own a house on Fifth Avenue, which is now a Japanese back scratcher emporium with Turkish rugs in the window, and their children go to Public School No. 86. But they are not happy.

Thus we find that the great Imky diamond has proved more of a liability than an asset. During the past ten years hard luck has become so much of a staple in this rare old family that they hardly notice it, and it was not until one of the little Imky girls read about the Evil Eye, which is supposed to watch over her relatives (she gets the Sunday papers before her father and takes out the funnies and most of the interesting sections and makes birds' nests out of them), that the present generation of Imkys realized that they were harboring a viper in their midst. It was then that they began to look for it. The first thing to do in getting rid of a viper is to find it. "First catch your viper," as Mark Twain said when told of reports of his death having been greatly exaggerated.

And so we find ourselves confronted, not only

by the problem disposing of the famous Imky diamond but of unearthing its whereabouts. If the Imky family could locate their trouble (and Mrs. Imky, as we have seen, has said that it must be somewhere about the house because she remembers having put it there herself) they could give it to the Salvation Army, for the Salvation Army just eats up hard luck. But, so far, like the salt mill in the fairy story which ground out salt even from the bottom of the sea, the Imky diamond, wherever it is, is grinding out headaches for its owners, and nobody can stop it. Perhaps the best thing for the Imky family to do would be just to stop having children and die out.

How to Break 90
in Croquet

WITH the complete collapse of golf and tennis as sports, owing to the upturn in business, more and more people are taking up the old-fashioned game of croquet. It is a daredevil, madcap sort of sport, it is true, but then, these are dangerous days.

Croquet has one big advantage over most other games in that it can be played nowhere except on a croquet-field, and, as there are practically no more croquet fields in existence, the number of possible players is limited. This lends an aristocratic air to the sport, and also makes it easily avoided. The curse of golf and tennis has been the difficulty in avoiding playing them.

Croquet is played on a smooth grassy field (or "scrudgeon"). The best croquet-scrudgeon in the world is said to be in Sydney, Australia, and is now used as the first floor of a house.

Nine wickets are stuck in the grass in various spots, so placed as to be easily tripped over by non-players crossing the field in the twilight.

The idea of the game is to knock a wooden ball through these wickets with a wooden mallet in such a manner as to make a loud clicking noise.

It will be seen, then, that in order to send the ball through the wicket, instead of to one side, the position or "stance," is very important. It is to your stance, or "position," that I will therefore devote this first lesson. Perhaps you will not need more than this one lesson.

Let us take the first shot which you will be called upon to make—through No. 1 wicket. As No. 1 wicket and No. 2 wicket are very close together, you ought to be able to go through them both at once, unless you have been drinking. (I naturally do not mean that you actually try to go through the wickets yourself—unless you have been drinking.)

For this first shot, I usually use the mallet called the "massie," because it has a blue band around it. Taking an easy grip on the handle with both hands something in the manner of a flute-player, only more virile, you bend over the ball, with the feet about two feet apart and both pointing in the same direction. ·

Here is where the beginner is apt to make his first mistake. In leaning over the ball, he is likely to lean too far, so that his hat drops off in front of him onto the ball. There is also danger

27

that, if he leans still farther, he will topple over forward himself, scratching himself quite badly on the wicket. This should definitely be avoided, as it is difficult to gauge your shots with a trickle of blood coming down into your eye from a small cut on your forehead.

He is likely to lean too far

After making sure that you are not leaning over too far (a point on which any friend will be glad to advise you) the thing to do is to bring the mallet back and then forward, hitting the ball a resounding thwack. Novices are apt to push the mallet, forward first and *then* bring it back, a maneuver which, although succeeding in hitting the ball, is *not* good croquet form and does not result in a very smart stroke. A good rule to remember is "Never *push* the ball through the wicket—unless you can do it on the sly with your foot."

Now, we have learned three things in this lesson: (1) do not lean over so far that you topple over or lose your hat, (2) do not let the nerve strain get you, and (3) do not talk to strangers.

The whole secret of a successful croquet-player is poise. I can not emphasize this too much—or maybe I have already. The acquiring of poise is aided by proper costuming. If you go out on a croquet field dressed in a white tie and tails, you may be *de rigueur* for a formal dinner, but, before you have played half way around the course, you will be conscious of the fact that you are *not* the best-dressed man on the croquet-field. This self-consciousness will impede your game and you may end up the laughing-stock of the sporting-world. This, I take it for granted, no one wants to be.

I would recommend a loose-fitting, rather vulgar, blazer of some awning material, giving free play to the arms and neck, and a smart

Unless you can do it on the sly with your foot

panting of flannel or duck, giving free play (fifteen cents on Saturdays) to the legs. This will ensure at least ease and comfort, so that, if you happen not to want to play any more croquet (as is quite likely after the first game) you may go and lie down without strangling to death.

(In our next lesson we will take up HOW TO GET THE BALL THROUGH THE WICKET WITHOUT CHEATING.)

What
Would Happen?

THE Sunday papers have recently been frightening us with special articles entitled: "If the Earth Suddenly Stopped Revolving" and "If the Earth Speeded Up Its Movements," showing, with colored pictures, just what these vagaries on the Earth's part would do to the Man in the Street, provided he could stay on the street.

This has set me to thinking. What do you suppose would happen if the earth were suddenly to speed up, then suddenly stop, then speed up, then stop, alternating the two maneuvers in fairly rapid succession and keeping it up as long as it got a laugh? What would happen to us then?

I have asked Dr. LeNoix, an eminent French scientist who happens to be sleeping across the foot of my bed this morning, and he has told me, in a general way, what the effect would be of such monkeyshines from Old Mother Earth. Following is a summary of his remarks:

If the earth were suddenly to speed up, the

first thing that would happen would be that everybody's buttons would fly off and everybody's feet would slip right out straight in front of them. Then, if it were suddenly to stop revolving, the buttons would fly back into place again (they would have to be resewed later when things had calmed down a bit) , and everyone in the world would swirl out into space. This might be fun, so long as everyone was doing it, but I should hate to be the only one. Just what else would happen wouldn't make much difference to us if we were all hurtling through space toward the sun, but if the earth were quick enough about starting again we would all snap back to earth, except those lightweights who had flown off too far to be caught by the force of gravitation. They would be just out of luck, that's all, and we needn't bother any more about them.

As long as the earth kept speeding and stopping, speeding and stopping, we should probably keep up flying off into space and dropping back again, all of which might become a little tiresome after the novelty had worn off. There would be a lot of giggling and joshing on the part of the younger folks, but anybody who had work to do or who was trying to catch up on his reading, would get pretty disgusted after a while, I should think.

There would also be a complete change in temperature every time the earth changed its tempo, freezing cold with glaciers one minute and burning hot the next. Polar bears would come down from the North during the cold periods and then have to rush back every few minutes to keep from being burned alive.

This is going to upset traffic no end, to have polar bears rushing back and forth on the north-and-south bound streets, especially as, at the same time, a lot of deep-sea animals will be crawling out of the ocean bed when all the water dries up. (I forgot to mention that the oceans will all dry up during the hot spells. Forgive me.)

Among the minor catastrophes which would result, would be the explosion of all watches in their owners' pockets, due to the impossibility of recording the quick changes in time, and the electrifying of all silver fillings in teeth, causing them to pick up radio programs and burn holes in the cheek. Everybody's shoe-laces would come undone and trip up the wearers, and it would be impossible to fry an egg anywhere near the way you like it. In short, hell would break loose.

Of course, if we were all bounding back and forth between the earth and the sun, it wouldn't make much difference about our watches exploding or our shoe-laces coming undone, but all the same, it wouldn't be a very comfortable feeling to know that these things were taking place. The whole thing would upset practically all routine life as we know it, and I, for one, am dead set against its happening at all.

But Dr. LeNoix says that he doesn't think we have to worry, not for a year or so anyway. He simply was giving scientific answers to my hypothetical questions, and I am a little sorry now that I asked it.

Filling
That Hiatus

THERE has already been enough advice written for hostesses and guests so that there should be no danger of toppling over forward into the wrong soup or getting into arguments as to which elbow belongs on which arm. The etiquette books have taken care of all that.

There is just one little detail of behavior at dinner parties which I have never seen touched upon, and which has given me personally some little embarrassment. I refer to the question of what to do during those little intervals when you find that both your right-hand and your left-hand partner are busily engaged in conversation with somebody else.

You have perhaps turned from what you felt to be a fascinating conversation (on your part) with your right-hand partner, turned only to snap away a rose bug which was charging on your butter from the table decorations or to refuse a helping of salad descending on you from the left, and when you turn back to your partner to continue your monologue, you

find that she is already vivaciously engaged on
the other side, a shift made with suspicious
alacrity, when you come to think it over. So
you wheel about to your left, only to find yourself confronted by the clasp of a necklace and
an expanse of sun-browned back. This leaves
you looking more or less straight in front of
you, with a roll in your hand and not very
much to do with your face. Should you sit and
cry softly to yourself, with your underlip stuck
out and tears coursing unnoticed down your
cheeks, or should you launch forth into a
bawdy solo, beating time with your knife and
fork?

Of course, the main thing is not to let your
hostess notice that you are disengaged, for, if
she spots you dawdling or looking into space,
she will either think that you have insulted
both your partners or else will feel responsible
for you herself and start a long-distance conversation which has no real basis except that of
emergency. So above all things you must spend
the hiatus acting as if you really were doing
something.

You can always make believe that you are
talking to the person opposite, making little
conversational faces and sounds into thin air,
nodding your head "Yes" or "No," and laugh-

ing politely every now and again, perhaps even continuing the talk from which you had been cut off, just as if someone were still listening to you. This may fool your hostess in case her glance happens to fall your way (and sometime we must take up the difficulty of talking to hostesses whose glances must, of necessity, be

You can always make believe that you are talking to the person opposite

roving up and down the board while you are trying to be funny) but it is going to confuse the person sitting opposite you in case he or she happens to catch your act. If one looks across the table and sees the man opposite laughing and talking straight ahead with no-body on the other end, one is naturally going to think that he had better not take any more to drink, or perhaps even that he had better not go out to any more parties until some good specialist has gone over him thoroughly. It is this danger of being misjudged which makes the imitation conversation inadvisable.

You can always get busily at work on the nuts in front of your plate, arranging them on the tablecloth in fancy patterns with simulated intensity which will make it look as if you were performing for somebody's benefit, especially if you keep looking up at an imaginary audience and smiling "See?" Even if you are caught at this, there is no way of checking up, for anyone of the dinner guests might possibly be looking at you while talking to somebody else. It isn't much fun, however, after the first five minutes.

If you have thought to bring along a bit of charcoal, you can draw little pictures on the back on either side of you, or lacking charcoal and the ability to draw, you might start smothering the nicer-looking back with kisses. This would, at least, get one of your partners to turn around—unless she happened to like it. As time wears on, and you still find yourself without anyone to talk to, you can start juggling your cutlery, beginning with a knife, fork, and spoon and working up to two of each, with perhaps a flower thrown in to make it harder. This ought to attract *some* attention.

Of course, there is always one last resort, and that is to slide quietly out of your chair and under the table, where you can either crawl

You can draw little pictures

about collecting slippers which have been kicked off, growling like a dog and frightening the more timid guests, or crawl out from the other side and go home. Perhaps this last would be best.

How Sheamus Coomara Met the Banshee

An Irish Folk Tale
with Notes

EXPLANATORY NOTE: *In any reading of Irish folk-lore it is well to know the meanings of the names which have, through the ages, been given to the fairies, or "the good people," as they are sometimes called. We must know, for example, that a Glaubie (from the Irish words* bhhobcht-t-bhhbean, *meaning "a cooper with no eyelashes") is a little man, usually seen alone, who is always cooping. He has no eyelashes, which probably is why he is always alone. The Glaubie is famous for pulling hairs out of the back of people's heads when they are stooping over gathering berries. A Mooka (*suggaun-t-seadhh, *meaning "the slightly throaty call of a singing-grass which grows only in the north of Carrigogungunniel") is a little woman, generally seen riding on a horse which has only one haunch, who sets up a wail similar to that of the singing-grass whenever anyone in the neighborhood is about to be sick. There is some question as to which comes first, the wail or the impulse to be sick, but most people who have seen her believe that the wail does it. Then there is the Lallow, or, if you are going to write it in Irish, the* Murrúgoigh morúadhh, *which*

41

is a sort of seagoing moth which travels in swarms. The Lallow is generally supposed once to have been a beautiful white bird which was changed into a princess and, not liking that so much, had itself changed into a moth, the moth being more of a nuisance. The Lallows follow ships and, it is believed, if the sailors knock their pipes against the rail so that the ashes fall on any of "the good people" who may be swimming by, the Lallows turn into drops of tar which fall on the decks, giving the sailors a hell of a job to clean them up.

These are just a few of the many varieties of Irish fairy, but they will serve to give you an idea of why they are called "the good people." The others we can take up as they enter our story.

SHEAMUS COOMARA was once as likely a lad as ever shaved a shillelagh [i.e., travelled from Cappagh to Sligo], drained a quart, or wore no necktie; fearing for nothing but the want of drink, caring for nothing but the kiss of a fine lass (bad cess to them), and thinking of nothing but finishing a sentence with three balanced phrases like these; drunk or sober, a kiss and a blow was the way of Sheamus Coomara, and a mighty foine [fine] way it is of either standing up or falling down. More is the pity that, through the means of his thinking, and drinking, and caring for nothing but dancing to the "Shan Van Vocht" [*an-t-seann-*

42

bhean bhoct], this same Sheamus Coomara fell into bad company; for surely "the good people" are as lousy company as anyone could come across in a day's journey from Aherlow to Dingle.

[*That will be just about enough of this kind of writing. From now on we'll take it easy.*]

Well, now, it so happened that Sheamus Coomara was going home one clear frosty night, singing a song he had heard, the chorus of which was all he could remember if his life depended on it:

> *"Rum fum boodle boo,*
> *Ripple dipple nitty dob;*
> *Dumboo doodle coo,*
> *Raffle taffle chittiboo!"*

[If you think I am just trying to be silly, I refer you to "Irish Fairy and Folk Tales," edited by W. B. Yeats, for the original of this song.]

Just as he was finishing the seventh identical chorus, he felt a crack on the back of his neck (for which you can hardly blame whoever gave it) and he was thrown forward on his chin while, at the same time, his legs were lifted high in the air and his trousers pulled off by the cuffs, following which he was rolled up in a ball, heels over head, and jammed into a prickly-briar bush [*sneidh suggaungh*].

"Ho, ho!" roared Sheamus Coomara, " 'tis one of *the good people!*" And with that he received a clout over the skull which left him senseless but happy. When he awoke, a little man in a black cap was bending over him, going through his pockets for money, of which, thanks to the living, and the drinking, and the wild thinking, of Sheamus Coomara, there was no more than you could put in the right eye of a *Lianhaun-sidhe* [a particularly small *leprechaun*].

"*Shu gu dheine?* [Who are you?]" asked Sheamus, fearing to know.

"I'm not tallink you," replied the Little Man, in a strange dialect.

"Are you a *thevshi* [ghost]?" asked Sheamus, trying hard to think where he had heard such talk before.

"Leesten, *goy*," said the Little Man. "I'm tallink you dun't esk kvestions, I'm eftch moneh!" And, with that, he raised his hand to strike again.

But Sheamus Coomara, by this time suspecting that this was not one of *the good people,* in spite of his pixie behavior, grabbed the Little Man under his strong right arm and carried

him off to the Magistrate, kicking and screaming.

"What's your name?" asked the Magistrate.

"Isador Lepidus," replied the Little Man.

"Well, I'll be a sogh-and-sogh," exclaimed
Sheamus Coomara. "A Jewish banshee!"

"What is your trade?" asked the Magistrate.

"I'm a gunman," said the Little Man.

"Sixty days in the *augh-ishka* [hoosgow],"
said the Magistrate.

And, from that day to this, the residents of
Sgeulaigheachia in general, and Sheamus Coomara in particular, always look twice when they
receive a clout on the side of the head to make
sure that it is really from one of "the good people" or just a gunman from New York. For,
taken all in all, they work much the same.

Rapping
the Wrapper!

PROGRESS is all right in its way and I
suppose that, if you have progressed as far
as you feel you can in one line, it is permissible
to try progressing in another. (I can't get arrested for saying *that*, certainly.)

There used to be an advertisement which
read: "We couldn't improve the product, so
we improved the wrapper." That's fine, provided you *do* improve the wrapper. But there
is such a thing as improving the wrapper so
that nobody can get at the product. It may be
a perfectly dandy wrapper, air-tight, water-
tight and germ-proof, but if the buyer has to
send it to a garage to get it off, something is
wrong somewhere.

I have just been trying to get at a roll of mints.
I bought them at a newsstand thinking that I
would slip one of them into my mouth before
meeting my wife. So I started clawing at the end
with one nail as I walked along. It was obviously
not the end to claw at. So I turned it over and
started on the other. That end had been clamped

46

I turned it over and started on the other

down by a stamping machine usually reserved for tinning sardines. I tried biting at both ends (one after the other, naturally) and gave up just before an inlay came out.

Now all that I wanted was a mint, mind you. If I had wanted to uncrate a piano or crack a safe

It broke into a hundred bits in the middle

I would have expected to go to some trouble. But when all a man wants is a mint just before he meets his wife, the least that he can ask is that the mint will go half way with him. These mints were out-and-out antagonistic.

I finally saw that it was a personal matter, and gave my whole attention to it. If it was a fight

48

they wanted, I was game. I stopped short on the sidewalk and laid my hat over a hydrant. I tried breaking the thing over my knee and hitting it against a building. (Round One. The mints.)

It finally ended by my dashing the whole business to the sidewalk as a child does a torpedo, with the result that it broke into a hundred bits. It broke into a hundred bits in the middle, but the two ends remained intact and as tightly clamped down as they had been when they left the foundry.

Now I don't have to have mints. It should be a case of you-treat-me-right-and-I'll-treat-you-right between me and the manufacturers. If it isn't going to be, I have other resources.

Good
Bison News

A VERY comforting fact was just called to my attention concerning bison, and I think that every comforting fact ought to be passed on these days. The bison of America are not, as we have always been led to believe, on the verge of extinction. On the contrary, the work for their conservation has been so successful that there are now too many bison.

All this has probably been common gossip among bison-fanciers for many months, but I have been out in the Far West where they don't go in much for this Nature business, and it was not until I returned to New York that I learned definitely that all was well with the American buffalo. In fact, the problem now is: "What to do with the extra ones?"

The last I heard about these shaggy beasts there were only a few of them left and those were dying off like flies. "Isn't it too bad about the bison?" everyone was saying, gloomily. "In ten years there won't be one left." Then the war came, and people got to thinking about other things, and, if you had come up to me last week and asked me if I wanted to see a bison I should have said: "Don't be silly! There are no more."

But very quietly for twenty-five years the American Bison Society has been working tooth and nail to save this noble breed of typical American animal, and they have done so well at their work that last year 1,400 surplus bison had to be killed. It would almost seem that they had overshot their mark.

Just how you would go about saving buffaloes from extinction I do not know, but, whatever the secret was, the American Bison Society certainly hit upon it. I suppose that the bison themselves had something to do with it, but they evidently hadn't quite got the knack of the thing before the American Bison Society came along.

The President of the Society is as much at sea as anyone else. "When we began conserving these animals," he is quoted as saying, "every one believed they would become extinct within a few years. It was simply a gesture on our part to keep alive as long as possible a memory of the Old West. But the buffalo did not die, as you see, and our problem now has become one of getting enough food and space for him."

51

It may have been just a gesture on the part of the American Bison Society, but it was a gesture that packed a punch. Evidently the bison took it seriously. Old West or New West, it is now fixed for bison for many years to come. In Canada alone last year there were 6,300 buffaloes, which was exactly 1,200 too many for the available standing space. Somebody has got to speak to them, in private, and tell them that a joke is a joke.

The thing goes more or less in a circle, for the income from the hides and meat of the bison which have to be killed to make room for the others, is used to provide food for the newcomers and their Indian caretakers. But it is rather a tough fate for a member of a proud breed, who thought he was being saved from extinction, to find himself being slaughtered to make room for others coming in. He might even ask, with perfect justice: "What is this— a gag?" It might almost have been more fun to have been a member of a rapidly disappearing species than to be hustled into an abattoir as "surplus stock."

But the memory of the Old West is in no danger of dying out, as far as bison are concerned, at any rate. And the American Bison Society has proven what can be done by putting your mind to it. The President says that all other big game are also increasing, with the exception of the mountain sheep. "I'm afraid his kind will be gone in a few years despite what we can do," he adds, sadly.

Fie! Those are defeatist words! What was done for the bison ought to be able to be done for the mountain sheep. Only this time it might be well to establish a quota.

Off to the City for the Week-End

OFF to the City for the week-end! What a thrill there is in that very phrase for the man and wife who have been spending every Saturday and Sunday in the country all summer! And how lucky the host who can open his cool town apartment to some poor family who would otherwise have to bake under the merciless Long Island or Westchester sun, writhing in wrappings of white flannel, struggling for breath under Colonial rooftrees, or searching in vain for damp spots of beach sand on which to sit without wincing. A host with such a haven at his command should know all the little refinements which will make a week-end visit to his apartment memorable beyond mere considerations of physical comfort. In other words, he must give the whole thing That Touch.

Week-ends in the City usually begin on Friday night—if the guests have anything to say about it. "Jack can come right up from the office," says the wife eagerly, "and I can get the 4:15 into town, or can drive in if the leather on the seats of the car is cool enough. At *your* apartment, then, at about a quarter to six?" It is well to be prepared from perhaps five o'clock on.

Friday evening in town is fairly easy for the host to map out. The guests, if arriving by train, can be met at the station by that old family retainer, the Red Cap, who is never late and never surly, and who, furthermore, is paid by the guests themselves and disappears from the scene immediately they are deposited in the luxurious taxi which is always waiting at the entrance to the station. No standing on the platform looking up and down for the family station wagon or hiring a local conveyance which smells like an old sleigh just out of the barn loft. Your guests are driven to your apartment in the best and fastest (certainly the fastest) that sixty cents can buy, and you don't have to worry about them until they are at your very door. Possibly you may not have to worry about them even then.

Of course, you will want to have the guest-room ready for them, and here is where the summer town host discloses himself as either a conventional dullard or a man with imagination. There is nothing so pleasing to an out-of-town guest as to come into his room, hot and dusty from the country, and find little evidences of consideration, little personal touches which show that it is really *his* room and not just "the guest-room." There is one feature of week-ending in the City which makes it easier for the host to arrange the guest-room. The guest is practically never in it. He takes possession of it on arriving, washes up, leaves his bag, and from then on is out on the town. Sometimes he doesn't even come back for his bag on Monday morning, having it sent directly to his office or back to the country some time later in the week. This simplifies things considerably for the host.

It is well, however, to be prepared for some contingency in which the room *may* be used for a few hours, for some guests from the country are in bad physical condition and may not be able to stand the complete gaff of an entire week-end without dozing off, or, at any rate, mixing up a few powders for themselves. It is wise, therefore, to have the room ready with bicarbonate, an ice-cooler, fruit salts, and perhaps even an electric vibrator. The bed, just as a matter of form, may be made up, but the counterpane should be removed, as any sleeping that may be done will be *on* the bed and not *in* it. There should be plenty of coathangers for use as imitation bows in burlesque ballets.

Books for the bedside table are an important item in making the guest feel at home. They should be chosen with the individual's preference in mind, of course, but there are three or four which are never out of place over a Saturday and Sunday in the City. "Practical Railway Painting and Lacquering," by Miskella; "Principles of Real Estate Appraising," by Zangerle; "Bicycling for Ladies," by M. E. Ward; "A Manual for Small Museums," by Coleman; and "The Culture and Diseases of the Sweet Potato," by Tannenhaus, are books which are always grateful to the tired guest who is hovering in the limbo of Slumberland after an evening in town. Your guest will thank you for having placed them by his bed, especially if, during the night, he happens to think that he sees something moving in the corner of the room, or if, as some guests often do, he wants to press ferns.

Now for the entertainment proper. For town entertaining exactly the opposite tactics from those in use in the country are indicated. The ideal host in the country allows his guests more or less to shift for themselves. That is, there should be no compulsion at any specified hour to play tennis, go riding, or swim up and down the front stairs. But in the City there should be a complete schedule made out in advance, with perhaps little copies of it made for the guests to refer to occasionally to see if they are running on time. Dinner on Friday night should be promptly at 11:30, or as near that time as the preliminaries are over. In case it is decided, as the evening wears on, that dinner is unnecessary, this time may be used for more preliminaries. A theatre party should be planned, and abandoned at the last moment. There are always a lot of plays during the summer which can be abandoned at the last moment, and there is nothing which gives a party so much satisfaction as to decide *not* to go to the theatre after all.

If your apartment is in a penthouse, your week-end problem is solved right there, except for the matter of finding guests who have climbed down into the street. It is always well to have a light of some sort on the ground floor to indicate to those unfamiliar with the terrain just where the re-entrance to the building is, and a few extra dollars to the elevator man will accustom him to the same guest appearing to be taken up several times in succession without ever having been taken down. Things like this are very likely to confuse elevator men unless they are forewarned.

In case the more agile guests do not feel like going back upstairs immediately, there is always the opportunity for fresh air and recreation, to say nothing of the indulgence of more

It is well to have three or four sets of the Sunday papers delivered

sporting instincts, in a ride around the Park in one of those victorias which are moored just off the Plaza Hotel. Victoria-riding is, and should be, one of the features of city week-ending, and two or three complete circuits of the winding parkways behind a smart-stepping steed at two or three miles an hour, should result in high good humor and perhaps a few boughs of hydrangea blossoms. If you play your cards right, you may even be able to persuade the driver to go home with you and perhaps bring the horse right up into the apartment, a never-failing source of amazement to the lazybones who have stayed behind playing backgammon.

If your apartment is not in a penthouse there are always penthouses which you may visit or even some where you may go as paying guests. Penthouses, however, are not essential, as along about ten in the evening a cool breeze always springs up from somewhere, especially from 52nd Street up, and the heat very seldom figures in the discomforts of a week-end in town. The cool breeze at the Puncheon is especially refreshing, especially with a little mint in it.

Sunday, whether it be in the country or in town, is always a difficult day for the host, as many of the guests can not be found and those who are on hand are in a rather ugly mood. In town the problem of missing guests is not so bothersome, however, for you can be pretty sure that they are somewhere safe like the police station or the Reference Room in the Public Library. There are so many places in New York which people who have been cooped up in the country all week have been longing to get at, that very often your entire group may take matters into their own hands and relieve you of any responsibility for their entertainment.

With those guests who stick and who show up on Sunday rather untractable, there is not much to be done. It is well to have three or four sets of the Sunday papers delivered so that each guest may have one rotogravure section to himself. He may not really be looking at the pictures, but he can at least hold the paper up in front of his face and be relieved of the necessity for conversation.

You need have no worry about what to feed any one on Sunday, unless perhaps your man wants to fix up a little paté of aspirin garnished with *cresson* (the *cresson* can be used as false mustaches by those who happen to be in jocular mood—if any). Unlike Sunday in the country, where every one feels obliged to sit in front of a large, heavy dinner with his eyes shut, the visitor in town should never be forced to sit still at a table for more than three minutes at a time. After Saturday, group eating on a town week-end party is definitely out and you can close up the kitchen for good until Monday night.

Along about four-thirty on Sunday afternoon begins the influx of people in tweeds and flannels who have sneaked off from country house-parties and driven in town for a few hours' relaxation. They have told their hosts that they are going out for a little drive, or perhaps a game of golf, and have immediately headed for town, where they will join you and your guests with tales of rural hardships. This will serve to cheer your own guests up and you can tell the visitors all about Friday and Saturday nights, making it sound even better than it was. Some of them, who have made a definite break with their country hosts by pleading an engagement in town for the evening, will stay with you all night, so really your own house-party loses its entity on Sunday evening and, as far as you are concerned, is over.

This little outline has, of necessity, been rather sketchy, and perhaps you have wondered what became of Saturday. So will your guests; and this, I take it, is the mark of a perfect holiday.

An Old Problem
Revived

I DON'T suppose that it is important enough to sidetrack any of the big issues for, but I wish that some of these psychological conferences would give a little thought some Saturday afternoon to the matter of those two little bits of paper that come off in our fingers the first time you try to pull a paper towel out of its box. They really call for attention.

The question of paper towels has been gone into many times by reformers, but I do not remember ever having seen the specific matter of those two little bits of paper covered. I need hardly rehearse the unpleasant details. Your hands are wet, you take hold of the two ends of the towel to pull it down, and all that you have are two little corners of wet paper stuck between your thumbs and forefingers.

What to do with them? That is what some conference has got to go into. A man can't handle a thing like that alone.

If you happen to be the dreamer type, like me, you may stand for hours holding out two

If you happen to be the dreamer type, like me

bits of paper for somebody to take off your fingers. Thwarted in getting out the whole towel, you may give in too easily to Fate and just wait there, brooding, until the paper dries and falls from your fingers of its own accord. By then your hands are probably dry, too, so there is no need for the towel at all.

If, however, you are not a defeatist, and believe in putting up a fight, you may set out determined not only to get the paper off your fingers but actually to get the rest of the towel out. This takes courage and quite a lot of planning and I admire the man who can go through with it. I must admit that I have, most times, walked out of the wash-room with wet hands and nothing but the two little pieces of paper between my fingers to remind me of my humiliating defeat.

Stronger men than I am, however, tell me that the way to get rid of the towel corners is to snap the fingers vigorously as if to an inaudible "ha-cha!" thereby disengaging the paper and freeing the fingers for a fresh attack on the towel. Or, for the less spectacular-minded, the fingers may be scraped against the wall of the wash-room in a quiet and dignified manner, with the same result. All that is needed, in any event, is a little initiative and get-up-and-go.

65

The whole matter, however, is a question for the psychologists, and I am sure that if I, and others like me who find themselves stymied by little things like bits of wet paper, were to go to a good clinic and put our problem squarely before experts, we would find that, after all, we had been making too big an issue of the thing.

Bright
Sayings of Parents

THERE have been so many columns of
newspaper type devoted to the bright
sayings of children that this one today will be
given over to contributions from children telling of cute remarks their parents have made.

Children have their pride, too, and are as
pleased as Punch when their fathers and
mothers come through with something really
observing or smart, instead of the usual par-
ental smooch.

Take, for example, the following contribu-
tion from Marian Wiltznitz, aged 12, of
1486754 Ocean Boulevard, Emporia, Kansas:

"Dear Cute Sayings of Parents Dept.—

"I was sitting in my room the other day tearing the
leg off a doll when my little father, aged 41, toddled in
and asked me if he could borrow five dollars until
Tuesday. 'Whatever do you want of five dollars, you old
rogue?' I asked him, between smiles. 'Who said anything about five dollars?' he snapped back. 'You did,
sonny,' I replied. 'Well then,' he said soberly, his brow
puckering into a frown and his upper plate dropping
with a click, 'have it your own way. Teacher said

67

today (he goes to Reform School) that we must all bring in something that we have caught, and I thought that I might catch that five dollars that your aunt gave you for Christmas.' He presented such a cute appearance, standing there in his football suit, that I couldn't bear to give him the money."

Or the following from George Welt, aged 7, of the United States Senate, Desk No. 9:

"My mother, who has been 29 for eight years and will have her 29th birthday next Friday, is quite a trial to us kids. She is always making us show off before strangers, many of whom are insane. She makes us recite, stand on our heads, and shoot at each other with bows and arrows, and then says, 'They never took a lesson in their lives.' You can see where this might get tiresome.

"So the other day we decided to get back at her, and when the guests began to come in, we hid in our room and blacked our faces with burnt cork. Pretty soon she began to call to us to come down and put on our act. One by one (there are two of us) we filed into the room, looking for all the world like two children with their faces covered with burned cork. The guests were aghast, or, if you like, the ghasts were aguest. Mother, however, took it like the trooper that she is. All she said was: 'I guess that my husband's children by his first wife must have come to visit us. Mine will be down in a minute.' Cute?"

As a topper, may we quote from a night-letter sent by Alfred Deedee, aged 3, of 45 Deedee Street, Deedee, D. D.:

"My mother and father, whose combined ages are enormous, say awfully entertaining things when they are together, which is every Wednesday. Last Wednesday they had me in stitches. Two stitches in my lower lip and four across my forehead.

"My father led off by asking my mother if she thought he was made of money. 'I am not sure what it is you are made of,' she replied, 'but I'm pretty sure it isn't money.' This amused my father so that he hauled off and topped her into the china-closet, much to the surprise of the cups and saucers.

"You should have heard that! Mother came out, smiling to keep the blood back, and said: 'Did you order those opium sets for the guest-room today?' My father did not answer. That was what I thought was so smart of him."

If *your* parents have said any cute things, or done any cute tricks, write in to this department, and if they are good enough to print, we will read them aloud to *our* parents, who get awfully restless along about five-thirty in the afternoon and like to be read to.

Elevator
Weather

TALKING about the weather is all very well if you are among friends and don't let the talk get rough, but it does seem as if we ought to draw the line somewhere. (Of course, this is only my personal opinion and I may be old-fashioned, but I would rather be old-fashioned than terribly, terribly ill with fever and have to wear ice-packs for weeks on end.)

I do think that we talk about the weather with a lot of people who don't know anything about it. For example (and it is the only one that I can think of at the moment), elevator-men. If there is one class of workers who are asked questions about the weather from morning until night it is the elevator-men. And if there is one class which knows absolutely nothing about the weather, it is also elevator-men. Let us see if this is not true.

The elevator-man, shall we say, gets into his elevator at eight o'clock in the morning. Unless he happens to be running the elevator in the Eiffel Tower or some other openwork structure he never sees the daylight again until he goes out to lunch. Next to stokers in an ocean liner there are no workers who have less opportunity to form an opinion on the weather. A tornado could appear on the horizon and sweep across town in a leisurely manner and disappear on the opposite horizon, and the elevator-man would never know—unless it happened to rip his building down.

And yet we come in from the outside, with an abundant supply of red-hot information on the subject, and the first thing we say to the elevator-man is: "What is it going to do—rain?"

And the elevator-man, either to humor us or because he feels himself to have some strange intuitive sense, replies: "It certainly looks like it."

If one wanted to heckle and be nasty, one might come back with: "*What* looks like it?" This would force him into an admission that he was basing his judgment on the appearance of the twelfth, fourteenth, and fifteenth floors as he shot past them. But that would be hardly fair to do, as we ourselves brought the matter up and led him into committing himself.

Did you ever stop to think that every person who gets into an elevator and finds himself alone with the operator makes some comment or asks

71

"What is it going to do—rain?"

some question concerning the weather outside? Did you ever stop to think what that means to the elevator-man? From eight until six he has no conversation addressed to him except that dealing with heat or cold, rain or shine.

On the first warm spring day, along about four in the afternoon, an elevator-man told me that he had said: "It certainly does!" just three hundred and twelve times in answer to people coming in from the outside and saying: "Well, it looks as if spring were here!"

"I am often tempted to deny it, sir," he said, with a wan look in his eye. "I am often tempted when they come out with 'Well, it looks as if spring were here,' to snap back at them and say: 'Oh, you think so, do you?' or 'That just shows all you know about it.' But what would be the good, sir? It would only confuse them, and there we should be."

I do feel, however, that something ought to be done, either to stop people from asking the elevator-man what the weather is going to be, or to keep him from answering as if he really knew. It is almost hopeless to keep people from asking. That is more of a reflex action on their parts, like twitching. One enters an elevator and one asks the man whether or not it is going to rain. It is purely physiological reaction, just as one winces slightly before entering a subway turnstile or ducks when going under the Brooklyn Bridge on a Fall River boat. There is no sense in starting a campaign to keep people from asking the elevator-man about the weather. The only thing to do is to discourage elevator-men from answering.

My plan would be this: Select a company of perhaps eight men to go about town from elevator to elevator. They assemble outside the building and run over their lines. The first one enters the elevator alone.

"Is it going to rain?" he asks the operator.

"It certainly looks like it," the operator will reply. So far, so good.

The next man comes in and takes the elevator on its next trip. "What is it going to do—snow?" he will ask.

"It certainly looks like it," the man will reply. But he will tremble a bit.

The third member of the conspiracy will enter with "Well, what is this—spring?"

"I guess it is," the man will venture. "It certainly feels like it."

NUMBER FOUR: "Are we getting a little more winter for a change?"

OPERATOR (*quite nervous by now*): "I guess

74

we are. It certainly—" (*Trailing off into nothing.*)

NUMBER FIVE: "Going to have a little thunderstorm?"

OPERATOR: "I shouldn't be surprised—from the way it looks." (By this time the operator would be surprised at nothing.)

And so this would go on, until all possible combinations of contradictory weather predictions had been exhausted and the operator had stopped his car between the sixth and seventh floors on the way down and burst out crying, refusing to go down to the ground floor again. This ought to put a stop to all this nonsense.

So why don't about seven or eight of us give over a couple of months to this reform? We could all have lunch at some quiet place and then start out, in high good humor, to settle the weather problem once and for all, at least as far as elevator-men are concerned.

Garbled
Favorites

A FEW nights ago I found myself, not very much to my surprise, singing in a loud voice from a pink song-sheet on which were printed the choruses to a batch of old-time favorites. There were lots of other people singing with me, so I could let go. I rather fancy myself at singing old-time favorites.

At least, I always had fancied myself, especially in the department of lyric-remembering. None of this "dum-de-dum-de-dum" for me. I sing the words right through from beginning to end, and have had many compliments on my memory. As yet no one has mentioned my voice, but I take that as a good sign.

However, on consulting the song-sheet (which I did more to humor the management than because I needed it) I was shocked to find that I have been singing the wrong words to many of my specialty numbers all these years. Not *all* wrong words, of course, but enough to make me stop and think.

I have, for example, been bellowing *In the*

Shade of the Old Apple Tree with considerable confidence for over a quarter of a century, sing-

Singing old-time favorites

ing the ante-penultimate line so that it made no sense:

> *I could hear the dull buzz of the bee,*
> *In the blossoms that you sent to me*

whereas, of course, it should be sung:

> *In the blossoms, as you said to me.*

I remember occasionally thinking that a bee in a nosegay was a bit out of place, but never stopped to consider also that, according to my version, the lady was sending the nosegay to the gent. In fact, the dangerous proximity of the bee had long ago ceased to worry me, and I have just been ploughing ahead, using my own version, and even teaching it to others. It rather frightens me when I think of it.

I have also been going hog-wild on *A Bird in a Gilded Cage,* singing "a pitiful sight" for "a beautiful sight," "she's not what she seems to be" for "she's not tho' she seems to be," and "she sold her soul for an old man's gold" for "her beauty was sold for an old man's gold."

In the last-mentioned mistake I have even been so cocky as to laugh to myself at the ignorance of the writer in rhyming "soul" and "gold." You can't be much more unfair than to distort a lyric-writer's words and then blame him for not making them rhyme.

In *Break the News to Mother* I have been so wrong as to be incoherent. I have transposed lines, putting "just say there is no other" up in Line One, and, when I found myself stymied in Line Three, just repeating "break the news to mother" for good measure.

The first line to *Daisy* I have sung "Daisy, Daisy, give me your answer true" instead of "give me your answer, do." In *I Want a Girl* I have insisted on "a dear old-fashioned girl with

78

eyes of blue" in place of the original "a good old-fashioned girl with heart so true." I have done those things which I ought not to have done and left undone those things which I ought to have done, and there is no health in me.

There is only one ray of hope for me in this song-sheet. According to it, the ante-penultimate line of *Yip-i-addy-i-ay* reads, "my heart wants to holler 'hurry'." Now, any printer who would set "hurry" for "hooray" is not infallible.

Possibly the whole song-sheet is wrong.

The
Curse of Efficiency

USUALLY I am a stickler for people being on the job and staying on the job until it is done. I am a strict taskmaster for myself, and I expect others to be equally strict in their attention to duty. (There will be a short wait until the laughter of my employers and friends has died down.)

But there are certain professions and trades in which I welcome inattention and slackness. I am even delighted when I find their representatives not on the job. The lazier they are and the more they soldier, the better I like it. "Never mind your duty," I would say to them. "Take all the time off that you want to."

To begin with a very obvious instance—is there anything more warming to the heart than a good, unreliable dentist? To have a dentist's secretary call up and say: "Dr. Merch is staying at home today and won't be able to keep that appointment"—does life offer many more satisfactory thrills?

The only trouble is that dentists, as a class,

are pretty conscientious and stick to their work like grim death. If they ever do get a hang-over, or suffer from inertia, they fight it off and are usually right there by the old chair at two-thirty precisely. I don't think that they know how little criticism there would be if they were

They are usually right there by the old chair

to relax every once in a while and take it easy. All work and no play, you know, Dr. Merch!

On my way to a washroom in a hotel or night club I am usually hoping that the brush-boy will not be there. I don't care what he is doing—he may be out drinking somewhere or robbing a store—so long as he is not on the job when I enter. If he comes in when I am half

way through washing my hands it doesn't count.
I grab my own towel, pull out the plug myself,
and push by him before he has a chance to take

I would pay boys just to stay outside

even one swing at me with his brush. I feel that
I have that right.

But if he happens to be one of those fanatics
for duty and is right on the spot when I enter,
arranging lilac-water and pushing pomade at
me, I am as putty in his hands. If I were run-

ning a washroom concession, I would pay boys well just to stay outside and talk with the coat-room girl the minute a patron appeared. I am sure that mine would be the most popular washroom in town.

On entering a book-store I am always re-lieved when no one comes up to me right away and asks me what I want. I could find a book store where a really lazy attendant stayed in the back room until I called him, or even had to go and drag him out, when I had found just what I wanted to buy, I would patronize it ex-clusively.

In fact, the book shop which I do patronize most has just this advantage. I don't think that the proprietor is lazy, but he must have a feel-ing that, for the first five minutes, a patron ap-preciates being neglected; for there have been times when I have browsed around among the books, made my selections and read several chapters of the first one, before he appears. But he is a man of rare sensitiveness and probably makes only half the money that he could if he were a hoverer or a pusher.

The same applies to headwaiters who take such an interest in your particular meal that you lose your appetite. I have never yet ordered a dish that a headwaiter suggested, and if, be-

fore I can stop them, they happen to suggest
everything on the menu, I order ham and eggs
out of spite.

To my mind, the ideal restaurant has no
waiters at all in sight when you enter and one

I have never yet ordered a dish a headwaiter suggested

never puts in an appearance until you have
mulled over the menu for at least five minutes.
I know that this is contrary to all rules of service, but I sometimes wonder if the people who
make rules for a trade have ever consulted the

patrons. If I were running a restaurant (after having gone bankrupt on my washroom) I would have a sign up reading: "If you want service, ask for it."

That there is something wrong with me in these respects, there can be no doubt. If I come home and find a message to call up someone who, I know, is ready to make some money for me, I am relieved if I find him out when I telephone. I am vaguely relieved when almost anybody is out when I telephone, whether I want to talk to him or not. This, of course, does not make sense. Neither does it make money. But, with money where it is today, who cares?

What Are Little Boys Made of?

DID you know that you have enough resin in your system to rub up a hundred violin A strings? Or enough linoleum to carpet two medium-sized rooms (without bath)? You were probably not aware of these valuable properties lying dormant in your physical make-up, and yet scientists tell us that they are there.

As you all were taught in school, our body is made up of millions and millions of tiny particles called the Solar System. These tiny particles are called "aeons," and it would take one of them fifteen million years to reach the sun if it ever broke loose and *wanted* to get to the sun.

Well, anyway, these millions and millions of tiny particles are composed of hydrogen, oxygen, iodine, phosphorus, Rhode Island, Connecticut. There is also a blue-plate dinner for those who don't like iodine. The action of all these elements sets up a ferment (C_2HN_4, or common table pepper) which sometimes ends in digestion but more often does not. If any one of these agents is lacking in our make-up, due to our having dressed in a hurry, we say we are "deficient," or perhaps we "feel awful." Even with everything working I don't feel so hot.

It is only recently that doctors have discovered that we have many more elements in our systems than was originally thought. Whether we have always had them and just didn't know it, or whether they were brought there and left by some people who wanted to get rid of them has not been decided.

They tell us that the average 150-pound body (and a very pretty way to phrase it, too) contains enough carbon alone to make 9,000 lead pencils (not one of them ever sharpened, probably).

Another item which the doctors tell us we have in abundance is hydrogen—"enough in excess," they put it, "to fill about a hundred child's balloons." There's a pretty picture for you! As if we didn't have troubles enough as it is, we must go about with the consciousness that we have the makings of one hundred child's balloons inside us, and that under the right conditions we might float right off our chairs and bounce against the ceiling until pulled down by friends!

Thinking of ourselves in terms of balloons, lead pencils, whitewash (we have enough lime

We might float right off our chairs

in us to whitewash a chicken coop, says one expert), and matches (we are fools to bother with those little paper books of matches, for we are carrying around enough phosphorus to make 2,200 match heads), all this rather makes a mockery of dressing up in evening clothes or brushing our hair. We might just as well get a good big truck and pile ourselves into it in the raw whenever we want to go anywhere, with perhaps some good burlap bags to keep the rain off. There is no sense in trying to look nice when all that is needed is a sandwich-board sign reading: "Anything on this counter—15 cents."

And that is the ultimate insult that these inventory hounds have offered us: they tell us just how much all this truck of which we are made is worth in dollars and cents. They didn't have to do that. Put all our bones, brains, muscles, nerves, and everything that goes into the composition of our bodies onto scales and, at the current market prices, the whole lot would bring just a little over a dollar. This is on the hoof, mind you. If we wanted to tie each element up in little packages with Japanese paper and ribbon, or if we went to the trouble to weather them up a bit and call them antiques, we might be able to ask a little more.

For example, the average body, such as might

meet another body comin' through the rye, contains only about one-tenth of a drop of tincture of iodine at any one time, and one-tenth of a drop would hardly be worth the dropper to pick it up for the retail trade. And yet, if we *don't* have that tenth of a drop something happens to our thyroid gland and we sit around the village grocery store all day saying "Nya-ya!" Or to our pituitary gland and we end up wearing a red coat in a circus, billed as Walter, the Cardiff Behemoth: Twice the Size of an Ordinary Man and Only Half as Bright.

I don't see why scientists couldn't have let us alone and not told us about this. There was a day when I could bounce out of bed with the lark (I sometimes let the lark get out first, just to shut the window and turn on the heat, but I wasn't far behind), plunge into a cold tub (with just a dash of warm to take off the chill), eat a hearty breakfast, and be off to work with a light heart.

But now I get out of bed very carefully, if at all, thinking of those 9,000 lead pencils which are inside me. Too much water seems to be a risk, with all that iron lying around loose. Exercise is out of the question when you consider 2,200 match heads which might jolt up against each other and start a very pretty blaze before you were halfway to work.

Suppose that we *are* as full of knicknacks as the doctors say. Why not let the whole matter drop and just forget about it? Now that they have put the thing into our heads, the only way to get it out is for some expert to issue a statement saying that everyone has been mistaken and that what we really are made of is a solid mechanism of unrustable cast iron and if anything goes wrong, just have a man come up from the garage and look it over.

Facing
Facsimiles

STUDENTS of handwriting (among whom I can hardly be numbered, being unable to read my own on a clear day) will find a folder full of field work in the collection of facsimiles of famous American documents and letters, edited by Edward C. Boykin and purchasable, I should think, at any facsimile-shop which has a bar no longer than twenty feet.

Here in one shallow box, each suitable for framing or for sending out through the mails, are twenty-five life-size papers in their original handwriting, ranging from the much-facsimiled Declaration of Independence (I would like to see that in just plain 12-point Roman type for once) to Aaron Burr's challenge to Hamilton. It makes up into quite a mass of handwriting.

Most of it needs translation, which Mr. Boykin has furnished in an accompanying key-booklet. Based on this evidence, some of our great soldiers and statesmen must face the suspicion of having been cockeyed while on duty.

For example, "Stonewall" Jackson's last message to General Lee before the Battle of Chancellorsville bears a striking resemblance to a check made out by a friend of mine at the Ha-Ha Club one night and returned by the bank as being too silly for commercial consideration. Granted that General Jackson wrote it during his celebrated "flank march," and even granting the possibility that he wrote it on horseback, or even while riding two horses at once, there still remains quite a lot to be explained.

There is also one from Andrew Jackson to his Secretary of War directing him to prepare for war against the nullifiers of South Carolina. President Jackson seemed to have a little better control than General Jackson, but from his chirography the Secretary of War would have been just as justified in cancelling the rubber-boot contracts as in proceeding against South Carolina. It was lucky that the War Department was hard by the White House, so that questions could be asked and explanations made, otherwise we might have been at war with France in 1832.

There is one letter which I would like to see included in a collection of this sort, although it never achieved national importance. I heard of it only a few days ago, but it strikes me as being one of the more charming of our historical memorabilia.

Two young ladies of my acquaintance, sisters, were recalling a treasure-chest of their grandmother's, which was brought out on all occasions during their childhood to regale the neighborhood children with evidences of their family's contacts with national and local affairs. Among the relics was what was always known as "the Lincoln letter," a document which was handed about and studied with considerable awe.

It was not until they discussed it a short time ago that the young ladies realized that "the Lincoln letter" was not written *from* Lincoln to their grandmother, but from their grandmother *to* Lincoln, and had never even been sent to the Great Emancipator.

The grandmother, approving of his humanitarian proclamation, had been moved to sit down and write him to that effect, but, possibly because it seemed too fine a piece of writing to let get out of her hands, had never got around to parting with it. And so "the Lincoln letter" was kept in the family archives, practically under glass, the envy of all outsiders and the most revered among the *lares* and *penates* of that particular household.

I will try and get a facsimile of "the Lincoln letter" for Mr. Boykin's second edition.

One
of Three

I WAS coming out from a wedding with a
couple of other ushers—well, it wasn't exactly the wedding, it was the wedding reception
—when an Ancient Mariner stoppeth me.

"You fellows go on ahead," I said. "I want to
talk with Grandpa here." So they went on
ahead.

"Well, graybeard loon," I said to the Ancient
Mariner, "what's on your mind?"

"Well, you cock-eyed pubert," he came back
at me, "I got a story for your paper. Do you
want to hear it or don't you?"

"I've got just four minutes before I pass
out," I said. "Let's sit down here on the curb.
And don't take as long as Coleridge did."

"You keep a civil tongue in your head, or I
won't talk." And with this he took off his beard
in order to get his sibilants out better, and
began:

"I had just returned from that trip I was
telling you about (I shall make no attempt to
do this in dialect, if you don't mind) when we

had that little trouble with the Albatross, and I was naturally a bit jumpy. Jumpy and pretty sore at albatrosses. As a general thing I like animals, but this one had gone too far. So I set about thinking as to how I could get back at one. I am more the vindictive type, in case it interests you."

"It doesn't," I said, "but go ahead."

"Well, I figured it out and I figured it out, and pretty soon I says to myself ——"

"I thought you weren't going to do this in dialect," I interrupted. "What kind of talk is 'I says to myself'?"

"Sorry. So I *said* to myself: 'Why must it be that a dead albatross brings bad luck to sailors? Why couldn't a dead sailor bring bad luck to an albatross? Why couldn't a sailor dog an albatross all over the world, daring him to take a shot and finally driving him crazy?' It seemed like a good idea for a way to avenge my mates, and, being a man of few words, I set about doing it.

"First, I had to find an albatross. We were in port at Salem at the time, so I goes—so I went, pardon me—down to Boston, where I heard there was an albatross-fancier, and picked out a nice, healthy bird who looked as if he might be fun to worry.

96

" 'Shall I wrap him up to take out, or will you eat him here?' the man asked me.

" 'I don't want him at all,' I said. 'Just turn him loose and I'll give him five minutes head-start.'

"So the man turned the albatross loose, and as he started out, I yelled at him: 'You're laughing now, you son of a sea-cook ——' "

"No nautical slang, if you please," I said. "Remember, you promised."

"Oke," said the Ancient Mariner, blushing furiously. "Well, anyway, I gave him a pretty nasty sendoff and told him I'd be seeing him. Then I got into a little Moth plane I had hired for the occasion and started out after him.

"He set out for Brazil, with me just behind him. Once I caught up with him close enough to yell: 'Remember, it's good luck to have a sailor following you!' "

" 'I heard different!' he yells back, but I could see that he was nervous. He tried to cut across to the sea, but I was right there behind him, jeering and pointing my finger at him, so he turned back inland and started flying low across to Peru. I had brought along a watch-man's rattle and some of those rubber Bronx-cheer things, which I kept blowing at him until he was pretty near crazy.

97

"Then I drew up on him again and yelled: 'You don't dare shoot me—you don't dare shoot me—'fraidy cat—'fraidy cat!' and he began biting his under lip and trying not to hear. By this time we were well out over the Pacific and he was in a rage.

"He came down at New Zealand and I made a pretty landing, just clipping his tail.

" 'Look here, sailor,' he said. 'I can stand just so much of this. Bad luck or no bad luck, I'll shoot you down, so help me Louis Agassiz.'

" 'Go ahead and shoot, you old albatross you,' I said. 'But you know what happens if you shoot a sailor that's following you, don't you?'

" 'In some states you get a bounty,' he said, trying to be flip.

" 'All right, buddie,' I said. 'Go ahead and get your bounty, if you don't care how you make your money. But you won't be in very good shape to enjoy it,' I said. And I made a face like a dead albatross, which frightened him—and frightened *me* a little, too."

I lifted the Ancient Mariner's beard from off his lap and held it up to his chin.

"Beards on!" I said. "Your four minutes are up, and you are definitely *not* holding my attention."

"Don't you want to hear how it all came out?" he asked, in a pleading voice.

"I am mildly interested to know what became of the albatross," I said, rising from the curb and adjusting my immaculate silk hat.

"I got him completely cowed," said the Ancient Mariner, "and he came back with me in the plane, half laughing and half crying at being let off so easily. I have him right here, in case you want to talk to him."

"Oh, no you don't!" I screamed, and ran like the south wind to catch up with my brother ushers.

"I have had the most amazing experience," I said to them, and told them the story practically word for word as I have told it to you, my dears.

Music
for Children

THERE is a generally accepted theory (except among the children themselves) that a child should be taught to play some musical instrument, so that, when he grows up, he will have at least one social grace, other than the ability to walk without tripping.

The "social grace" angle is all right, I suppose, although there is very little parlor entertaining done in these days; but my idea in teaching a child to make music of some sort or other would be to make it possible for him to soothe his own savage breast when he is alone. A child who has been trained to play the triangle and sandpapers is going to have a rather thin time of it when he feels like a little solitary harmony.

Anyone who can play the piano or the guitar or the zither, or even the harp (if he can arrange to have a harp lying about conveniently at those places where he might want to strum to himself), is sitting pretty when it comes to self-solace. He can sit at the piano and play a few soft chords, or thumb out a simple routine in G sharp on the guitar and hum "Aloah" to himself, and pretty soon he will be crying just as hard as if he had paid good money to go to a movie or the theatre.

But what can a man do alone with a B flat cornet when his spirit craves music? He can blare out some notes, it is true and, if he is really a cornet-lover, may get a certain amount of satisfaction in blaring them correctly, but there is no spiritual salve in the process. On the contrary, he will probably get a series of knockings on the walls and ceiling of his apartment, and a query over the telephone as to where the hell he thinks he is—in the army?

Even a man alone with a saxophone has to be pretty much in love to work up any kind of sadness for himself in the privacy of his own room. And if there is any more meagre fare for the spirit than a wheezing from a single flute, I have yet to hear it—and I have heard some pretty meagre spiritual fare in my day.

The first instrument that I "took lessons on" was the banjo. Not the little, short-necked, combination banjo and mandolin of today, but the original Negro instrument with the long neck and five strings, one of which was always broken.

There is no spiritual salve in the process

In those days, there was no such thing as walking into a music store and buying a banjo part for the latest popular tune. You had to wait until somebody called "The Banjo King" had made a special arrangement in five flats, and as "The Banjo King" never got around to his arranging until two or three years after a number had died down, the result was that I had nothing to play but "The Return of the Jolly Haymakers" and the "Cream City Patrol."

And, even after the five-flat adaptation had been published, I couldn't play it with anybody else, because the piano arrangement was always in a different key. So I just sat at home and plunked at polkas and barn-dances from a book called "Fifty Musical Gems, Especially Arranged for the Banjo."

Things are made easier for banjo-players nowadays, I guess, and those with a mandolin finger-board you can even play from a piano score. But I have always wished that I had taken piano, or even guitar, lessons, so that I could sit in the twilight and make myself miserable. And I suppose that most pianists wish that they could play the banjo and mandolin the way I do. That's the way it goes. Never satisfied.

So, by all means, teach the child to play a musical instrument; but, if possible, bear in mind that he is not always going to be playing in a band, and may, once in a while, want to make a little music for himself in any key he happens to feel like at the moment. And teach him to play an instrument that he doesn't have to hold in his mouth, for he may want to hum "Aloah" to his own accompaniment.

The Chinese Situation

With "The Good Pulitzer Earth" being made into both a movie and a play (which means six imitations in each field if it proves successful), to say nothing of Mrs. Pearl Buck's going right ahead and *bringing descendants of old Wang into the publishing world, just as if there were plenty of food to go around, it looks as if we were in for a good, old-fashioned Chinese winter.*

Before the thing has gone too far (which it will), let us see just how far it can go. EDITOR'S NOTE: *Owing to the subsequent failure of the play and the postponement of the movie until next year, it went no further than the following parody.*

IT WAS the birthday of Whang the Gong. Whang the Gong was the son of Whang the Old Man, and the brother of Whang the Rich and of Auld Whang Syne. He was very poor and had only the tops of old Chinese wives to eat, but in his soul he was very proud and in his heart he knew that he was the son of old Whang Lung who had won the Pulitzer Prize for the Hop-Sing-and-Jump.

Now Whang the Gong, although he was known far and wide among the local missionaries as a heathen, had read enough of the Gospels to know the value of short words and the effectiveness of the use of the word "and." And so Whang the Gong spoke, and it was good. Good for fifty cents a word.

Now Whang the Gong awoke on the morning of his birthday, and opened one eye, and it was not good, so he shut it again. And he opened the other eye, and it was worse than the first. So the young man shook his head wilfully and said: "I will open no more eyes until the harvest comes." Now the harvest was full six months away, which gave the young man a hell of a lot of leeway, and he rolled over again and slept.

But Rum Blossom, the wife of Whang the Gong, did not sleep. At four in the morning, before even the kine had begun to low or the water to run in the tub, Rum Blossom had rubbed her small hand over her small eyes, and it was not good. It was lousy. She arose, then, and went into the pump-house.

"Excuse," she said to nobody in particular, as nobody in particular was listening to her words,

106

"excuse—I am going to have a baby." So she went into the pump-house, and, while the waffles were cooking, she had a baby, and it was a man. Which was pretty good, when you consider that it was born between waffles.

Now the winter wore on, and it was still the birthday of Whang the Gong, for Whang the Gong liked birthdays, for birthdays are holidays and holidays are good. And Rum Blossom, his wife, came to him and said, lowering her eyes as she pulled the stump of an old tree and threw it into the wood-box, "I am going to have another baby." And Whang the Gong said: "That is up to you." And he rolled over and shut another eye, which was his third, kept especially for shutting. So Rum Blossom went into the library and had another baby. And it was a woman, or slave, baby, which, in China, is not so hot.

"I will scream your shame to the whole village," said Whang the Gong when he had heard of the incident. "Yesterday you had a man child, which was good. Today you have a girl, which is bitterness upon my head and the taste of aloes in my mouth." And he repeated it over and over, such being the biblical style, "I will tell the village—I will tell the village." And Rum Blossom, his wife, said: "All right. Go ahead and tell the village. Only get up out of bed, at any rate. And get your old man up out of bed, too. I am sick of seeing him around, doing nothing."

And Whang the Gong got up out of his bed, and got his old man up out of his bed, all of which made but little difference.

He went without reply then to the wall and felt for the roughness which was the mark of his clothes-closet, and he removed the clod of earth which fastened it. "I will have my cutaway," he said, and went then back to bed. And Rum Blossom his wife came to him and said:

"I will get you your cutaway just as soon as I have had a child," and going into the clothes-closet, she had a child and came out with the cutaway. "Here," she said, "is your cutaway. Take it and like it." And Whang the Gong took it, and liked it, for it was a good cutaway.

It seemed as though once the gods turn against a man they will not consider him again. The rains, which should have come in the early summer, withheld themselves until the fifteenth of October, which was the date for Rum Blossom to have another baby.

And Whang the Gong said to Whang Lung, the old man his father, "How come? We have no rain." And Whang the Old Man said, "True, you have no rain. But you have babies galore. One may not ask everything."

And Whang the Gong was stumped. "A baby is but a baby," he said in confusion. "But rain is rain." All of which made no sense, but sounded good.

But the Old Man would hear none of his son's sophistry, and mouthed his gums, which were of tutti-frutti, and rolled in the grass, only there was no grass and so the Old Man rolled in the stones and bruised himself quite badly. But all this meant nothing to Whang the Gong, for three moons had passed since he had eaten nothing but spinach and his eyes were on those of Lettuce, the Coat Room Girl.

There was a day when Whang the Gong awoke and saw his wife, Rum Blossom, pacing up and down the room, but, as the room was only three paces long, the effect was unimpressive.

"Another baby, I suppose?" said Whang the Gong, shutting both eyes.

"Not so that you could notice it," replied his wife, in extremest pique. "I'm through." And there was that in her pique which allowed no come-back, and Whang the Gong knew that she was indeed through, which was O.K. with him.

And when pay-day came, Whang the Gong arose and put on his finest silken suit with an extra pair of pants and married Lettuce the Coat Room Girl, making two wives for Whang the Gong, one, Rum Blossom, to keep the books, and one, Lettuce the Coat Room Girl, to be the mother of his children. Which made it very simple, so simple that every one watching, smiled.

The
Vanishing Father

I T IS perhaps a little late in the day to be asking, but whatever became of the old-fashioned Pater Familias, the father who packed a punch? He was one of the bulldog breed, whose word was law, and when he rumbled in to breakfast all the boys and girls, to say nothing of Mumsie, threw themselves up against the wall and saluted. Being a father in those days was a job that called for a West Point training.

Today the entire breed of fathers seems to have gone sissy. They are lucky if they get what the rest of the family gets to eat and, as for personality, they might as well be the man who holds the tray for a magician. And it isn't so much because the rest of the family have got more self-confident (although a certain suspicion of poise has crept into the young folks lately), but the fathers have definitely turned yellow as a class.

The day that fathers stopped wearing side-burns and high-buttoned coats, they began to

*The day that fathers stopped wearing side-burns they
began to lose ground*

lose ground. A man in a soft-collared shirt can't expect to rate much respect, especially if the ends of his four-in-hand look like a lasso and he still tries to dress like a junior in college. The custom of carrying gold-headed canes was also a big help to building up a following. The men in the old days weren't afraid to rig themselves up in the regulation father's uniform, even to the extent of a Prince Albert on Sundays, and, as a result, they both looked and felt the part. It is this trying to keep young-looking that has put the father-racket on the rocks.

Along with this fear of looking like a father has come a fear of acting like a father. Fathers today are a craven lot when it comes to appearing in public as a parent. They try to wheel the baby-carriage up side streets and, if they are caught leading a toddler along by the hand, they try to make believe that they are minding the child for some strange woman who has just disappeared. I have even seen a father hurriedly slip a cigar into his son's mouth at the approach of friends, hoping that they will think he is out with a midget business acquaintance.

My
Achilles Heel

I WOULD be much more active in rioting and picketing than I am if I were not so absolutely certain of being hit on the side of the neck with a flying missile. This is not just fraidy-cat guess work on my part. I *know* that I should be hit, and exactly where.

This conviction of vulnerability on my part comes of years and years of being hit in exactly the same spot by flying missiles—up until now, chiefly snow-balls. Ever since I was old enough to go out alone into the snow I have always been the one who got hit on the side of the neck, just back of the right ear.

It made no difference where the snow fight was. If it was on the next block, behind a house, and I was simply walking along on my way to school, somehow a large snowball would weave its way around corners and through an alley and land just back of my right ear, where it would disintegrate and slip down under my collar. Next to the feeling of being spanked, the feeling of a snow-ball hitting and going down my neck is the most familiar of childhood.

Of course, when I was so rash as actually to be taking part in a fight myself, I took it for granted that I was going to be hit there, and engaged in my end of the war-maneuvers with my right shoulder hunched up in anticipation, thereby making myself one of the least efficient marksmen on my side. And, if someone in the opposing army didn't manage to catch me on my Achilles heel, one of my own mates saw to it that his arm slipped or that he mistook me for an enemy. And I got my socking just the same.

I never got hit anywhere else. I wouldn't have minded that so much. It was that constant assault, year in and year out, on the side of my neck just under the right ear that made a coward out of me.

Then came the age when I no longer engaged personally in snow-battles, and should, according to the insurance laws of averages, have felt exempt from being a risk. But I still get hit when I pass a snow fight. And it is still in the same spot.

When I enter a block in which boys are throwing snowballs, that same old instinctive hunching up of the right shoulder overtakes me. The boys may be on my left, but the missile comes from the right, by whatever devious ways a snowball may come at its command.

*That same old instinctive hunching up of the right
shoulder overtakes me*

I walk along, pretending not to see the engagement, but I know that, before I am out of range, a stray ice-pack is coming hurtling through the air, either by design or chance, and that I am going through the humiliating experience of being an older man hit by a small boy's snowball. And on the right side of the neck, just below the ear.

So, when it comes time for me to clamber onto the barricade I suppose that I shall do so, but it will be with my right shoulder hunched up against the inevitable missile, which, I am afraid, will not be a snow-ball. Until then, I keep under cover as much as possible.

Divorce
in the U. S.

IF THE movement toward a uniform national divorce law is to gain any headway it is necessary for everyone to know just what the quickest ways of getting a divorce are at present—and then discard them. The final plan must be as unsatisfactory as possible, in order that there shall be fewer divorces and more axe-murders.

I have, therefore, compiled a little outline, giving some typical divorce cases throughout the country, so that we may see what the best people are doing in those circles where marital unhappiness is a pleasure and where a man and his wife do not necessarily make a fetish out of domesticity.

These cases may not all be on the records, but each one sounds like something I have heard somewhere. You can't expect a compendium like this to be absolutely accurate in every detail.

In New York State, of course, getting a divorce is rather difficult. One of the parties must have decapitated the other with a knife no shorter than three inches, and must have severed the head clean from the body. Penknife jobs do not count, as they do not show premeditation.

In other sections of the country, however, the laws are less paternalistic. For instance, in Illinois a man recently got a divorce from his wife because she was always standing in front of the mirror just when he got around to tying his tie. He was a short man, and, although he tried standing on tip-toe and craning from left to right, he never could seem to find a spot in the mirror which was not full of his wife.

Once he even tried shooting her in the back, but she just leaned forward on her elbows and rested on the bureau until she felt better, and then went on with her primping. Even in the courtroom the husband's tie was still untied, and he asked to use the mirror in the magistrate's dressing-room. When he got there the magistrate's wife was there, fixing her hair; so the magistrate divorced *his* wife, too, on the same bill of lading.

In Arkansas, in 1911, a woman claimed that her husband looked at her queerly. "I don't know," she said, "it was just queerly. That's all I can explain it. Every once in a while he would look at me over his paper while I was talking to him. It was horrible, and I was unable to fulfil my social duties and became an object of commiseration in the community, if that's what you call it." The divorce was granted on the ground of "looking queerly at the plaintiff."

An interesting case occurred in Hawaii in 1905. That is, it was interesting in Hawaii in 1905. A wife sued for divorce, claiming that her husband would never get up off the floor, and the husband entered a countersuit claiming that his wife would never get down on the floor. "She was always walking around," he said. The husband was accorded the divorce on the ground of incompatibility.

Probably the most remarkable of all divorce cases in recent years occurred in Arizona in 1926 when a woman sued for divorce claiming that her husband had deserted her, taking with him their herd of cattle and silo. The husband did not contest the action and, in fact, could not be found, and as the woman obviously did not have a herd of cattle or a silo she was awarded the divorce. It later turned out that she had had no husband, either, having never been married. "I must have been drunk when I did it," she said, giggling.

Now, if we can only co-ordinate these cases, and others like them, and strike some average of justice and equity, we may be able to work out some national divorce law which will make it possible for everyone to be perfectly miserable.

Black
Magic

I N THE hurly-burly of modern life I sometimes wonder if enough attention is paid to
the old-fashioned rites of demonology. We have
tried almost everything else to get ourselves out
of the jam that we got ourselves into, but it
never seems to occur to anyone that a little
polite attention, accompanied by incantations
and a sprinkling of wolfsbane in the general
direction of several of the more influential
demons, might work wonders.

I have been experimenting in a small way
with the Black Arts, and, although I can't say
that I really have got any results that I could
take before the American Demoniacal Society,
I have messed up quite a few pots and pans and
driven the people out of the apartment next
door. That's a beginning anyway.

The particular demons that I have been trying to get into contact with is known to demon-
fanciers as Heidi (possibly a contraction of
Heidi-Heidi-Ho), and I will know him when
I see him, according to the books, because he

has the body of a scarlet griffin and the head of a four-eyed horse. That ought not to be difficult to spot.

The chief trouble with my experiments in bringing Heidi to light centers around my cat. I can't seem to get the cat into the spirit of the thing. In fact, I am just about ready to face the fact that I have got the wrong cat for my experiments.

According to the book which I am going by (Dr. Bataille's "Lucifer, the Boy and Man") I have done everything else strictly according to formula. Last night I shut myself in my room with the kitten and lighted a candle in a red globe. I drew a circle with a radius of twelve feet around the cat and myself.

I then plunged a dagger through a wafer which I had bought at the waferer's in the next block, a wafer which he assured me had been stolen at midnight from a Buddhist temple. This fascinated the cat, who immediately started to play with the pieces. Several minutes were lost recovering them and reprimanding the cat.

Following this I took a copper pot and filled it with some crystals which the druggist had fixed up for me after a formula in the book and placed the whole thing over the flame of my electric stove. A rather nice fog began to fill the room and an odor similar to that of burning oatmeal. (I have since found out that it *was* oatmeal.) On top of this I threw the claws of an owl, bought at the taxidermist's, and an old raincoat button. Practically nothing happened.

Then came the important part of the brew, which was to be three hairs from the cat's tail. By this time the cat was well out of the circle again and romping with its ball, which I had neglected to hide. I tip-toed stealthily after it, but it was so darned cute that I have to give the whole thing up and lie on the floor rolling the ball back and forth.

So there I am, no nearer bringing my demon to light than I was when I started, except for a rather nasty mess in the copper pot. Tomorrow I am going to get a good black cat, but I am a little embarrassed to go into the taxidermist's again and ask for more owl's claws.

Wind

SOMEONE has just estimated that the velocity of the wind on some of the stars is 140,000 miles an hour. That's too fast for wind to blow.

When you consider that what we call a "hurricane" is only between 75 and 100 miles an hour, you will see that 140,000 miles an hour is almost ridiculous. It could blow 1,000 miles an hour and still be the best wind in the business, but when it gets to going 140,000, it is just making a monkey of itself.

I would be terrified in a 140,000-mile-an-hour wind. I am terrified even in a full gale. I am not frightened about being blown over, for I am quite a big boy now and can hold my own against a pretty strong wind. But there is something sinister about a force that you can't even see. If the wind is full of snow or rain, I like it, and often button my pajamas up tight around my neck and go out for a walk in it. But when it just comes at you as invisible wind, I get a little panicky.

And yet there is a fascination about being

terrified that sends me out on deck when the
blow is at its height. I would much rather be
cowering below with the bed-clothes over my
head, but some masochistic streak in me makes
me push my way right up into the bow, where
I stand, gasping for breath and wondering how

I push my way right up into the bow

long it will be before she is blown right back
on her hind legs and all are tipped back off over
the taff-rail. "How fast is she blowing?" I ask
passing sailors, hoping that they won't answer,
for if they tell me that it is anything above
forty, my breath goes entirely.

126

It's that breath taking quality about a high wind that gets me down. I can't even take one of those warm-air blowers that barbers dry your face off with. In the old days, when I had some idea that a facial clay-pack drew the blood from the top of your head and made you feel a little better (an old dipsomaniac told me that it was just the thing), I used to lie there in the chair, looking like Bert Williams, and tremble with apprehension when I heard the air-blower being wheeled into place.

"Not too close to the nose," I would caution the barber (why is it that the impersonal article is always used to barbers? It is never "my nose," but "the nose," or "the moustache" or "the neck.")

But, no matter where he aimed it, the full blast found "the" nostrils, and I ended up by breathing in ten convulsive breaths a second, with never a chance for an exhale. Panic followed, and I usually found myself standing out on the floor beside the chair, gasping and rolling my eyes, a man one inch removed from suffocation and in full realization of the fact. It always ended by the barber fanning me for the rest of the process, and with a very small fan, too.

Going head-on into a high wind does the same thing to me, all in-take and no out-go; and yet I keep going head-on into high winds. I court panic and suffocation. But I guess that if I were to get on one of those stars where the wind is blowing 140,000 miles an hour, I would learn my lesson. I'll bet I'd lose my hat, anyway.

The Drift
to One Eye

AS IF the Future weren't full enough of
bugbears as it is, along comes a noted eye-
specialist and tells us that our eyes are growing
gradually closer together, so that some time
there will be just one big eye in the middle of
our face. It does sometimes seem as if it were
hardly worth while putting up the fight,
doesn't it?

First, there is the probability that taxes will
be higher before they are lower, then that there
will be another war, then that there will be
more taxes to pay for that war, and then, as the
last straw, that our eyes will grow closer together until they form just one big eye. What
provision, if any, is the NRA making against
this catastrophe?

Of course, according to the eye-specialist
(Dr. Shastid, of Duluth, whose paper in the
Phi Beta Kappa magazine I am not going to
pretend I read. I am not even on the mailing
list. I got my information from Time), it will
take some years for this unpleasant change to

take place in the human physiognomy. "Count-less ages" is the way he puts it, and that ought to let most of us out.

But before the actual change from two eyes to one occurs (and that will be a morning, when a man wakes up and finds himself with only one large eye!) there will have to be all that disagreeable period of preliminary narrowing of the bridge of the nose, with the eyes getting closer and closer together, and that might very well come within our day. My eyes are so close together as they are that I bet that I win. I bet that I am the first one-eyed man in the world.

But, with everybody headed for the same fate, it won't be quite so bad. Nobody can make personal cracks at anyone else, because the entire human race will be in the same fix. No one of your dear intimates can come up to you and say: "My! Aren't your eyes getting close together!" without your having the right to say back at him: "Have you looked at yourself lately?" Being only one unit in a world-wide anthropological trend has its compensations.

It is not a very pretty picture that Dr. Shastid paints, however. "In distant centuries or millenaries man will be a Cyclops, a Polyphemus, a being with one eye only. That eye, however, will not be situated in the center of the forehead. It will stand instead in the center of the face. The forehead will be much higher and the face below the forehead much shorter, and, at the horizontal boundary between the two, in the center of that boundary, the spot where now the bridge of the nose appears, there will stand the one great eye."

That, you will admit, calls for quite a readjustment of our present ideas of what constitutes a face. I suppose that it is because we have got so used to the old-fashioned face that this lay-out does not seem particularly attractive. It might be better to begin all over again, if we are going that far, and just do away with the face entirely and call it something else.

No mention is made of what becomes of the nose and mouth under this new-fangled plan, but I suppose that they, too, will be shifted somewhere else, possibly to the back of the neck. There certainly isn't much provision made for moustaches unless they are worn on the forehead.

But there! We don't have to worry about all this quite yet. The main thing is not to get panicky. Probably the worst that will happen to anyone alive today is that his two eyes will get to just barely touching at the corners. So just forget about it for a while and when it does come, take it like a man with a stiff upper-lip—provided you have any upper-lip left.

Pleasures
of the Senses

WE HAVE been brought up to consider pleasures of the senses as somehow ignoble. A sensualist is a naughty man, and don't let anyone tell you different. Just look at his face. It is sensual.

And yet all pleasures of the senses need not be anti-social, or even expensive. Wine, Women and Song may run into money and eventually give a man a sensuous look, but there are many other minor stimulants which are almost equally pleasurable, and which may be indulged in with no loss of self-respect and certainly no noticeable change in features.

With advancing age and a slight tendency to obesity, I have learned to concentrate on several of these less spectacular forms of sense-titillation, thereby leaving myself time for a certain number of civic duties and a contemplation of things of the spirit.

For example, I derive considerable sensual pleasure from lifting off a milk-bottle cap with some small pointed instrument like a pin or an

I derive considerable sensual pleasure from lifting off
a milk-bottle cap

awl, especially if it resists just a bit around the edges and does not end by splashing into the milk. I find that the greatest pleasure is experienced when the cap is exactly half off, but the final release is worth waiting for. There is a minor excitement in pressing the cap back on, especially if it has not become bent during the removal.

Somewhat the same effect, only on a slightly larger scale, may be gained by pulling the meat from the body of a lobster with an oyster fork. The fork should be inserted at the tip of the tail and the head (the lobster's head) held firmly in the left hand. Then lift slowly and carefully with the fork, using just enough force to extract the meat in a whole piece, but not enough to get the process over with at one tug. Just very gradually lift the fork so that the entire lump of lobster meat is disengaged inch by inch, leaving the shell absolutely bare. It really is magnificent.

Unwrapping the tin foil from a piece of cream cheese furnishes a tactile pleasure of a high order which is marred only by the difficulty of getting it all off. Executed slowly and carefully, however, the satisfaction derived from the first two-thirds of the wrapping process makes up for the anti-climax of having to pick out the bits of remaining tin foil with a fork.

Lest you think that I am concerned only with the preparation of foodstuffs in my search for pleasures of the senses, I will say that I have often been reduced to the point of swooning by the sensation of holding a book of just the right size and smoothness in my right hand. A pocket edition, about four and a half by six and a half, printed in ten-point Goudy and possibly two hundred and fifty pages thick, is a delight to hold and gaze at, even though it be written in an unfamiliar language. Surely no one could criticize this little indulgence or point a finger of scorn at the sensualist who seeks it out.

In this same class I would place a fresh copy of a well-printed Sunday newspaper before it has been torn apart by the women of the family. If, by any chance, it can be picked up whole from an outdoor front porch, still cool to the touch from the winter air, it takes its place among the major contributions to life's excitement. I would prefer that the "funnies" be on the inside. To be completely effective, a smooth, eight-column news-section should be on top.

Among other nice things to hold in the right hand are the butt of a Colt automatic (preferably unloaded), the warm bowl of a pipe, a round cake of soap, and a smooth stone held in position for skipping across the surface of a pond. The sight of the stone skipping is not bad, either.

Whitewashing a good board fence, applying lather with a shaving brush, snapping the clasps on a well-filled suitcase and puncturing a cellophane top to a bottle need no explanation from me, I am sure. The pop of a single-piece stud through the hole in the front of a dress-shirt is a pleasure reserved for men and those considerate wives who put their husbands' studs in for them.

There are, of course, hundreds of other little pleasures in life which I have omitted, and probably hundreds more which I have never experienced. But so long as I have those few which I have listed, and such others as Nature has in store for me, I shall not fear that my fires become completely banked or that life will lose its zest. And think of the money I shall be saving!

Route Nationale 14

How to Motor from Cherbourg to Antibes via Cherbourg

COME with me and we will motor through Sunny France, from the tippity-tip of Cherbourg to the top-*tip*pity-tip of Cap d'Antibes! Or come with me and we will go over to Dinty Moore's on Forty-sixth Street for some spareribs and sauerkraut. Anyway, we'll do *some*thing!

If it's motoring through France we're going, we shall have to get started earlier. We shall also have to have a motor. Perhaps we had better decide right now on Dinty Moore's.

To motor pleasantly from Cherbourg to Antibes, it is preferable to use one's own car, as in a rented French limousine the driver's mustache is always too big and too black. There really isn't much worry involved in taking your own car, unless you happen to be watching while they are lowering it down from the ship to the tender. Furthermore, in your own car,

you don't care so much what the children do
to the back seat.

THE ARRIVAL

On arriving at the port of Cherbourg you
are met on the tender by a representative of the
A.A.A. who will tell you that your license-
plates have just barely not arrived yet, but that
they will be in tomorrow *très de bonne heure*
(along about noon). So this means spending
the first night of your motoring trip in Cherbourg (Grand Hotel du Casino, or behind the
barrels on the new pier). Anywhere you stay,
you get to know Cherbourg.

While roaming the streets of this quaint old
seaport town (Napoleon said of it: *"J'avais
résolu de rénouveller à Cherbourg les merveilles de l'Egypte,"* but he didn't quite make
it, doubtless due to the lack of Egyptians), one
can see much that is of interest—to the Cher-
bourgians. One may also *be* seen and pointed
out as a native by the boat-train passengers as
they roll slowly through the Main Street.
("Look, Harry," they say, "at those picturesque
old natives! Don't those people *ever* bathe, do
you suppose?") One can also get a line on the
boat-train passengers themselves from the outside. They don't shape up so hot, either.

(Beauty note: Every woman looking out at the windows of the incoming boat-train has just been freshly lip-sticked in preparation for embarkation.)

A good place to spend the evening while waiting in Cherbourg is not the Café de Paris across the bridge. It isn't much fun in the Grand Hotel du Casino, either. But you are all excitement at the prospect of your early start in the morning, so it's early to bed, after a chat with the quaint old negro concierge from Philadelphia, Pa.

At seven o'clock you are up and ready, with everything strapped on the car and the children buried in the back seat under the extra hampers and coats. (One child is buried so deeply that he is a great big boy by the time he is remembered and dug out.) The maps are spread open and a schedule arranged which calls for lunch at Lisieux. (Hotel France et Espagne. Bad Martinis.) A light rain is falling.

At the *mairie* it will be found that the license-plates have not yet come, and eighteen shoulders will be shrugged. The car will then be driven back to the hotel (Grand Hotel du Casino, 100 fr.) and a more thorough tour made of

CHERBOURG (¼ kms.). A quaint seaport

town, of which Napoleon once said: *"J'avais résolu de rénouveller à Cherbourg les merveilles de l'Egypte."* It was his intention to revive in Cherbourg the marvels of Egypt, is the way it looks. You may see a statue of Napoleon in the public square across the bridge. On the other hand, you may not. You may also see Pauline Frederick in "The Woman Thou Gavest Me," the film for which was found in an old bureau drawer by the exhibitor. Then there is always the Café de Paris. And the Grand Hotel du Casino.

The license-plates not having come at fifteen o'clock, it is decided to spend the night in

CHERBOURG (¼ kms.) . A quaint seaport town which Napoleon once designated as the place where he was to revive the marvels of Egypt. To this end he appointed Vauban, the great engineer, to construct fortifications and plan a harbor which should be impregnable. (You learn a little more each day you stay in Cherbourg. By the time I left I was being groomed as Opposition candidate for Mayor. I was letter-perfect in the opposition, but my age was against me.)

During the second evening in Cherbourg, after seeing that everything is going all right at the Café de Paris, you can read up on the rules of the road, some of the most readable being:

1. In France one keeps to the right, except when skidding.

2. Danger signals along the road are represented by black triangles with little pictures on them. Be careful not to become so interested in looking at the pictures that you forget the danger. A picture of two little hills side by side (these French!) means *cassis*, or a gully across the road (Cassis, in vermouth form, also makes a nice gully across the road if taken in sufficient quantities). A cute little gate means a *passage à niveau gardé* or protected level crossing. An even cuter choo-choo (if you are traveling with children), with smoke and everything, means an unprotected level crossing. This is the one you mustn't get too fascinated by.

3. The way to say "dust clip of front hub" is *"ressort cache poussière de moyeu avant,"* something you really don't have to learn as you can always point. In case you end up in Holland the way to say it is *"Sluitveerje der smeeropening,"* which is just plain silly.

4. Gasoline is sold by the *bidon*. Be careful about this.

5. An automobile tourist arriving in France on March first for a four months' visit will take

out a *laissez-passer* for thirty days. This immediately puts the tourist under suspicion in the eyes of all officials and sometimes ends in his incarceration.

By this time it is bedtime, as you have to make an early start in the morning. There are very tall hat-racks in each bedroom of the Grand Hotel du Casino, from which you may hang yourself if you have to stay a third day in Cherbourg.

Up at seven, in a light rain. A chat with the colored concierge from Philadelphia, one last look around at the Café de Paris, a visit to Napoleon's monument to make sure what it was he hoped to make out of Cherbourg, and, at eleven o'clock sharp a trip to the *mairie* where there is tremendous excitement owing to the arrival of the license-plates. By this time you have made such friends with every one in the place, including the Mayor, that it costs you three hundred francs in tips. The adjusting of the plates, the signing of the Peace Treaty, the shaking hands and the shaking-down, take an hour and a half, so it is decided to have lunch at the

GRAND HOTEL DU CASINO (35 fr.) . A quaint old hostelry situated hard by the *quai* overlook-

ing the harbor fortifications built for Napoleon
by Vauban, the great engineer.

The Start

Leaving Cherbourg, believe it or not, we
ascend a gentle grade along winding roads
through picturesque Normandy (light rain).
The excitement of actually riding in a moving
automobile proves too much for the children
and a stop has to be made just this side of

Bayeux, famous for its tapestry and cathe-
dral, neither of which we see. The excitement
of passing through a French town other than
Cherbourg is too much for the children and
another stop has to be made just the other side
of

Bayeux, famous for its tapestry and cathe-
dral, although there was a perfectly good hotel
(Hotel de Luxembourg) on the way through.
At this point it is discovered that the "funnies,"
bought in an American newspaper the day before in Cherbourg, have been packed in a suitcase on the trunk rack, necessitating taking the
car apart to get them. From here on the children are engrossed in reading American "funnies," which gives us quite a stretch without a
stop to

Caen (pronounced "Kong"), famous as being the first train-stop from Cherbourg, to Paris, where most American tourists think they are in Cayenne.

Stop for the night at LISIEUX (scheduled for lunch the day before). Hotel France et Es-

Engrossed in reading American "funnies"

pagne. (Bad Martinis.) The residents of Lisieux sleep all day in order to be abroad all night under the windows of the Hotel France et Espagne (under the window of Room 34 in particular), where they walk up and down in an especially whittled type of sabot, pinching children to make them cry. Some also carry small horns or attach even smaller ones to bicycles, thereby effecting a squeak in synchronization with the bicycle wheels. This causes the fox-terriers (an exceptionally repulsive breed, fat and soiled) to bark, which, in turn, causes the children to cry.

Up at four (bad Martinis) and on the road at five-thirty, passing through such interesting towns as Évreux, Mantes, Flins, and St. Germain-en-Laye, none of which are seen owing to the entire family catching up on last night's sleep.

We are awakened by the sound of heavy traffic and, on inquiring where we are, are told that we are in Paris (Porte Maillot).

Here ends the first stage of our automobile tour from Cherbourg to Antibes. The stay in Paris is regulated by the length of time it takes to recover the use of our limbs and have the *ressort cache poussière de moyeu avant* fixed. The number of remaining checks in the A. B. A. book has also something to do with it.

CONTINUATION OF TOUR

(Paris to Antibes)

The P.L.M. train (*Wagon Lits*) leaves Paris (Gare de Lyons) at 19:40, arriving at Cannes at 11:02 the next day. Fifteen minutes motor trip to Cap d'Antibes.

My Personal Beaver

I HESITATE to mention the matter here, as I may be misjudged, and it really is something which concerns me, and me alone. Or so my lawyer says. But I simply have got to tell someone about my beaver. It is getting to be more than just a nuisance.

I call it a beaver, but that is really giving it the breaks. That is ascribing to it some definite shape and personality, and these things it definitely has not got. It hasn't got one single attribute that I like. All that I know about it is (and my lawyer tells me that I must be very careful not to say anything against it that I cannot prove in a court of law) that it keeps appearing in my house, or rather disappearing in my house. It is always darting around corners just as I look up, or behind beams just as I look down. It is this ability on its part to be either on the floor or on the ceiling which makes me think that it might possibly *not* be a beaver. No beaver that I ever heard of could dart around a beam on my ceiling.

It has, however, certain characteristics of a

beaver; it is rather round and dark, and seems to have a broad, flat tail, although I would not swear to the tail. It might be a smaller animal of the same type following it. (Good night, I hope not! If there were two of them I *should* be discouraged.) But if it is a beaver, it is a rather old and lethargic one and one who ought easily be caught up with except that I have no desire whatsoever to catch up with it. "Live and let live" is all I ask.

I first noticed it one day when I was feeling rather rocky after a night of moving three buildings from one place to another. (They weren't placed right at all, and so we tore them down and built them where we thought they ought to be. That sort of thing wears a man down.) I was looking at a strip of bacon with just about as dirty a look as anyone ever gave to a strip of bacon, when, glancing up to see if there might not be something in the bookcase that I would like to eat better, I saw this small animal disappearing behind the door. Now, I have not owned a small animal since my Scottie was arrested for inciting to riot in Union Square, and I have no friends who are small enough to dart behind a door 'way down there. So I naturally looked quickly away again, and thought nothing

148

more of the matter, except to pace up and down the room all day in a cold sweat.

The next day I was weaving on a tapestry which I am trying to finish for the museum at Bayeux, when, on glancing up at the ceiling to try to think of which stitch came next, I saw the

I saw this small animal disappearing behind the door

same small form whisk behind a beam, with just a suggestion of a tail protruding behind it. The tail was what made me say instantly to myself: "A beaver!" The ceiling was what made me say almost immediately afterward: "Beaver, my eye!"

This has gone on now for several weeks and

I am frankly at a point where I would cry if anyone pointed a finger at me. I asked my lawyer what to do about it, and he said to say nothing to anybody, but to lie low. But you can't have a stray beaver around the house, on the floor *and* on the ceiling, without telling somebody. But not a word more will you get out of me.

Who Killed Alfred Robin?

O NE of the myriad traits which distinguishes me from the nation's Great Men is my inability to finish a detective story. I can get right up to the last ten pages, but there galloping indifference sets in and I go out to the ice-box.

I can go for the first part of a detective story, where they are tripping over corpses and guilty-looking characters, and I perspire like a good one during the middle portions when screams and pistol shots are ringing out like chimes and Scotland Yard is biting its nails. But when it comes time for everything to be cleared up, and the detective explains just why he came to the conclusion that Scarboro did it I suddenly realize that I don't even know what the characters' names are, and that, furthermore, I don't particularly care.

I think that it is this question of characters' names that throws me off. As the story progresses, and more and more strange people are introduced, I get a little slovenly about filing them in my memory. I can't retain more than about five names, and, beyond that, I just trust to luck that I shall remember who they are when they come up again. Consequently, when I come to six solid pages at the end of the book which contain nothing but McCarthys, Wallaces, Martissis and Waldheims I naturally am at a disadvantage.

Following, if you are at all interested, is what the last ten pages of most detective stories seem like to me:

"Well, tell me, Inspector, what made you first suspect that it was Reedy and not Peroni who was at Balinto's place that night?"

"It was fairly simple, once we had established the fact that Gilgo could not possibly have been in Chicago with the Matessi gang. O'Rourke and Bleeker we knew were hard up —Greggory told us that—and Maude Marston had been working Dominic to get him to double-cross Vancy. *Now*—on the night when Freebish was seen coming out of Honfnagle's apartment ——"

"But it was McCorck who was seen, wasn't it? That was what Teemy reported."

"Teemy reported it because he was afraid that if Clark knew that Noglatz had been playing around with Elsie he would tip off the Gorelli bunch and Szcynocyz would squeal."

"Then you didn't positively know that Glack was in the tannery that night?"

"I suspected it, but it wasn't until we found the pawn ticket in Vanderhook's overcoat that we knew that Duchy was in with Levine and Sabisty. Alice Gratz knew, but she couldn't talk because she was afraid of McNamara."

"But what about the insurance policy?"

"The insurance policy, if you will remember, was made out to Osterville, and the dog belonged to Pasterson. It was the dog that really gave the whole thing away."

"Well, I'll be darned!"

"No, I wouldn't say that exactly. But you'll buy me a drink."

I know that it is a peculiar lack of concentration on my part that makes me so susceptible to brain-fag at the end of detective stories, for millions of people the world over seem able to remember characters' names and to react when they appear in the printed page.

But, so long as I get a certain amount of simple-minded enjoyment out of the first chapters, when the murder is committed, and can follow along with my forefinger over the more exciting developments of the plot, what difference does it make who really committed the crime? If I don't care, who does? It's my book, and I may do with it as I like.

The
Care of Fish

THERE is hope for all of us in the sporadic revival, with high social sanction, of what used to be considered strictly bourgeois pleasures.

When I was a little boy, for instance, one played backgammon only when one had tonsillitis and could find a disengaged aunt. Today backgammon is more *au fait* than sex.

And recently we find ourselves confronted with the necessity for keeping fish in an aquarium if we would be up-to-the-minute in pet culture. This must surprise the fish quite as much as it does some of us old fish-keepers.

We used to keep goldfish in my day, but we never thought of it as a particularly tony feat. We just had some fish, that was all. Everyone else in the neighborhood had fish, and the thing was more or less taken for granted.

And, by the way, I don't remember whatever became of those goldfish of ours. I suppose that they just got lost, but you'd think that you would remember what you did with a whole aquarium of goldfish. I must look around for them when I get home. They must be pretty old fish by now.

But the new fish that people are going in for now are not just the old-fashioned goldfish. They are fancy Japanese bull-fish and Turkish canary-fish, and little fish with faces like Mussolini who scowl at you through the glass. Instead of your watching the fish swim by as we used to, these fancy fish watch you. They come right up to the glass and follow you around with their eyes. I frankly don't like it.

But, if people don't mind being watched all day by a fish, and want to go in for keeping them, I suppose that we ought to spread as much information as possible about the care and feeding of fish, especially during this cold weather. You don't want a lot of *enrhumés* fish, coughing and sneezing around an aquarium.

In the first place, you must remember that fish are very stupid, and have to be told everything at least twice. There is one fish in particular (not to mention names) which has no forehead at all, and which doesn't even pay attention. If you have one of these in your aquarium, you are in for a rather discouraging time of it, I am afraid. You will just have to make up your mind to pamper it, and mustn't expect anything in return for your troubles. There is no pet as ungrateful as a fish, I am sorry to say.

First: the water that your fish swim in must be of just the right temperature. This is very important. A thermometer is useful in keeping it warm enough, but a better way is for you yourself to get into the aquarium first and test the temperature. If it is warm enough for you, it is warm enough for the fish.

Second: Never give them rich, starchy foods, for their little stomachs are very delicate. In fact, some of them seem to have no stomachs at all—just tails and heads. This makes feeding them quite a problem.

Third: Give them plenty of exercise. This can be done by going right up to the glass while they are looking at you and looking back at them, making just as ugly faces as they are making at you. If necessary you can say: "Boo!" or "Scram!" but with enough venom in it to make them realize that you mean business and are master of the situation.

They will then swim quickly to the back of the tank, and come back for more. If you keep this up long enough, they will get quite a lot of exercise swimming back and forth, and you will get a certain amount of satisfaction, too.

If this is not enough, and your fish seem to

be putting on weight and getting loggy, take the whole aquarium, fish and all, out on horseback through the park. Fish love horseback-riding, if it is done with someone that they love and trust.

Fish love horseback-riding

This sounds as if it were a lot of trouble to keep fish. It is. One solution to the whole problem is not to keep any fish at all. You may sacrifice a little something of social prestige, but you, at least, have your time to yourself.

"Awake, Awake!"

THE art of awakening people out of a
sound sleep is one which needs a little re-
fining. There is too much cruelty abroad. Being
awakened at all is bad enough without having
it done by a gorilla.

I don't suppose we should blame the Pullman porter because he gives those four vicious
tugs at the bottom of your blanket. When it
happens, I could leap from my berth and stran-
gle him with my bare hands, but, as I lie there
determining to go back to sleep just to spite
him, I realize that of all people, Pullman por-
ters have a right to be peremptory in their signals that it is time to get up. With a whole car-
ful of sleepers to whip into shape, they must
have a pretty tough time of it.

Sometime I would like to read an article by
a Pullman porter detailing the responses—and
percentage of direct successes—he gets on his
morning rounds. There is a man who sees human nature at its worst.

But, granting the porter's right to make a

158

beast of himself at awakening his charges, who else is justified in being uncharitable about the act? Certainly not friends or relatives of the sleeper. And yet among these we find the worst offenders.

There are some people who undergo a complete change of nature when it comes time to get someone else out of bed. Ordinarily they may be sweet-natured, considerate Christians, loath to offend and slow to command. But when the time comes to awaken somebody, a fiendish gleam comes into their eyes and their hands twitch in anticipation.

"Let me get him up," they sometimes beg. "I'll do it." Two fangs appear over their under lips and a hump on their backs, and they tiptoe to the bedroom where the unsuspecting victim is lying, like vampires on some grisly errand.

"Come on, come on!" they shout with glee. "Time to get up!" With this, and before the sleeper has a chance to scowl and gag himself into consciousness, they yank the covers back or shake him violently by the shoulder. The late Jack Pickford had a little whimsey of firing a revolver off in the room of the sleeper. This I do not consider one-tenth as despicable as the personal attacks of those who pretend that they are doing only their duty. A revolver fired to awaken a man is definitely a violation of all codes, a thing so horrendous as almost to be funny. There is no pretense of being anything but a cad of the first water, and I am not so sure that, if awakening has got to be performed, a

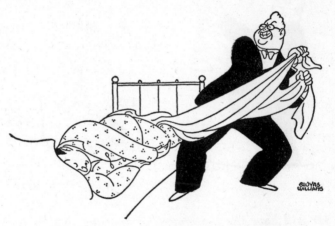

"Come on, come on!" they shout with glee

good revolver shot by the ear is not the kindest method to adopt. At any rate, the sleeper doesn't have those first awful seconds when he thinks that maybe, if he were to pretend to be dead, he would eventually be let alone. He knows that he is dead.

160

But the hypocrites who, already being awake, cannot bear to see anyone else sleeping, and yet have not the nerve to shoot a gun off, but must pretend that they are doing it for your own good —these are the abominations. As they leer down at you, after their vicious "Come on!" so smug

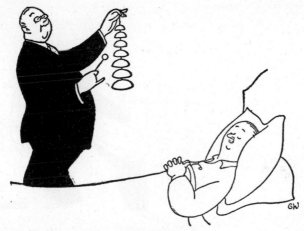

He will have the consolation of knowing that he has behaved like a gentleman

in their superiority and so sure that they are "doing the right thing," they represent the worst element in our civilization—the Brother's Keeper.

If anyone feels that he has to awaken me, I would suggest that he purchase a set of those mellifluous dinner chimes or a small harp, and walk slowly up and down beside my bed, playing something that he knows how to play. It may take a few minutes to bring me to, or it may take a couple of hours, but he will at least have the consolation of knowing that he has behaved like a gentleman and not an unconscionable boor.

And, besides, why does anyone feel that he has to awaken me at all? Did I ever ask to be awakened?

Bargains

I N THESE days of rising prices it is good to learn of one department in which we can still go plunging ahead at the old rates. The apparatus for collecting and preserving butterflies is just about where it was the last time you looked into the market. Butterfly collectors, attention!

In a catalogue issued by Watkins & Doncaster, 36 Strand, London, there is a list of all sorts of impedimenta dear to the heart of the entomologist rapscallion. And at such bargains! You'll fall over backward when you read them. You can get your sugaring net and your net forceps for Hymenopterists for 4/6 apiece and your zinc relaxing box (7 in. by 4 in.) for 3/-. If you want something larger than 7 by 4 in which to relax, there is always the hotel lobby or even a roadside bank.

Relaxing is a very important part of butterfly hunting, for you can push the human machine just so far then it breaks down on you. I suppose that relaxing box for a really large man would run well into 10/-, but it would be worth it.

A pupa digger (in leather sheath) comes for around 4/-, but I have no doubt that, if you don't mind carrying your pupa digger around without a sheath (and most people lose their pupa digger sheaths the first day out—I know that I do) you could get it for quite a bit less. A pupa digger is for digging pupas (otherwise why call it that?) and not for show. So let's forget the leather sheath and call the price 2/6.

Under the catalogue-head of "Setting Houses" we find that an "Entomologist's Companion" costs £5/10/6. It all depends on how lonely you get on a butterfly-hunt, whether or not you want to go to this expense.

A good companion is cheap at £5, especially one from a setting house, if you are the chummy type and want someone to talk to, but, if you go after your butterflies more or less seriously and rush about a lot, a companion would be in the way. When you get home with your specimens there will be plenty of time to gab, and you can probably get someone at home for nothing. Suppose we save £5 right here!

There is a very good book called "Novitatae Macrolepidoptera" by a German, Otto Bang-Haas (probably burned by now in the Nazi Renaissance) which is a catalogue of all the

Palaearctic Lepidoptera not contained in Seitz
Vols. 1-4.

You must have often wanted some sort of
catalogue of Palaearctic Lepidoptera not contained in Seitz Vols. 1-4, and here it is. The
only catch is that it will set you back 45/-, and
that is no small item. It might almost be better
to struggle along on Seitz Vols. 1-4 and make
up the rest as you go along. Suppose you don't
know exactly *all* the Palaearctic Lepidoptera in
the world. What's the worst that can happen
to you?

Don't think that Watkins & Doncaster deal
only in the apparatus of butterfly-catching. You
can buy direct from them a real Malvae Griz-
zled Skipper for 0/1 or a Pudibunda Pal Tus-
sock for /2, or the egg of a Temminck's Stint
(in case you go for birds' eggs) for the absurd
sum of 2/-. And a good taxidermist will know
what I mean when I say that a whole Taxidermist's Companion, equipped with brain scoop
and pricker, is worth every shilling of the 15
charged.

Of course, with the dollar rushing up and
down as it is, this is not a very good time to be
dabbing in pounds, shillings and pence, but if
you will just set this list aside until things get
settled again, you can order a bundle from

Watkins & Doncaster which will make anybody's Christmas one to be remembered.

I am thinking of getting a brain scoop for
myself right now, regardless of the dollar. I figure that I would be saving money.

Naming
Our Flowers

I WONDER how many of us who pretend to love the flowers really know how they got their names. I do not mean their Latin names, because nobody knows where they got those, not even the people who named them. Somebody was just in a silly mood, that was all.

But, for instance, how did the "double-gaited wertroot" come to be called that, instead of "Winkle Peter-in-Bed"? What is there in the history of "Walmsley's cowlick" that makes it necessary to call it "Walmsley's cowlick"? Wouldn't it be fascinating to know the ins and outs of flower nomenclature? Perhaps "fascinating" is too strong a word. Let us rather say "awful."

There is a legend concerning the "Crazy Kitty, or MacNerty's fields-awash" which more or less clears up the mystery of its name. It seems that the flower was originally known as "sauerkraut," because it grew to just the height of a pig's knuckle. Near a certain field in which it grew in abundance lived an old witch who was known to her intimates as "Crazy Kitty," because her name was Kitty and she was as crazy as a coot. There can be no doubt as to how Crazy Kitty got *her* name.

It seems that this old woman had a particular dislike for the flower called "sauerkraut" and used to say that if the darned thing came up next Spring as abundantly as it had in the past she would move from the neighborhood. She said this every Spring.

It was this particular dislike of Crazy Kitty's for the charming flower that caused the boys of the town to call it after her, and when she learned that her name had been applied to her pet aversion she went through the streets one night and set fire to every house, practically wiping out the community. And so the flower came to be known as "Crazy Kitty" the world over in her honor. Just why it is also sometimes called "MacNerty's fields-awash" has never been cleared up.

It has always been considered a delicate compliment to name a new and lovely flower after the wife, mother or sweetheart of the originator, which accounts for some otherwise unaccountable names, such as the "Mrs. Sam Cyzcyzocyz rose," "the Assistant Secretary of Public Works Lilian D. Wratch begonia" and

"the Emma Grobdigger Naumglatz primrose."
It was in honor of five little girls that the "La-
pino Country Day School Basketball Team
knee-action violet" became known as such.

We have only scratched the surface of the
study of flowers' names, and it ought to heal
right over, if we take care of it. My own
method of designation is to point to the flower
that strikes my fancy and say, "Give me a dozen
of those yellow ones."

How
to Eat

NOT only does it look as if we were in for
an era of expert wine-tasting-and-spill-
ing, with connoisseurs hanging over our shoulders to make sure that our Chambertin 1921 is
just exactly the temperature of somebody's
body, but, along with it, we are being made
food-conscious.

The gourmets and food experts are now in
the saddle, and a man can't pick up his paper
or magazine without reading the bad news that,
all his life, he has been eating his cup-custard
like a barbarian, and that the old *maître d'hotel*
at Foyot's used to say that anyone who would
eat cup-custard without a dash of *kirsch* over
it, and a few chives, slightly warmed, needled
into the top crust, would sell his grandmother
to a river-boat captain.

With all the people there are who claim to
know all about special eating tricks it is very
funny that one strikes so few dishes which are
really knockouts. All my life I have been going
from place to place to get legendary dishes that

170

are supposed to make me swoon the minute they are passed under my nose, and all my life I have been pretending to be bowled over by them. As a matter of fact I have been able to take practically all of them in my stride.

"Just go to this little place in the Rue Felix Potin," I am constantly being told, "and tell Jean that Mr. Gerbish sent you, and that he is to fix you up one of those special fish and kidney tarts. He'll understand." So I go and tell Jean, and he understands, and the fish and kidney tart is brought in, under motorcycle escort with all sirens blowing and everybody else in the restaurant backed into the corners.

Well, it's all right. That's usually the best that can be said for it. But it seldom is anything to make you fall flat on your face about. Even if, as Mr. Gerbish told you, you hold one mouthful of it for half a minute, and drip four dashes of Angostura bitters and a quarter of a teaspoonful of melted butter into one corner of your mouth, and a sip of 1844 Madeira into the other corner of your mouth at the same time—it is still just fish and kidneys, and no better than any good fish and kidneys ought to be. Sometimes it isn't even as good.

I once went to dinner with an old gentleman who was famous throughout New England for his steak sauces. He wouldn't let the restaurant do anything but bring the steak to the table, along with eighteen or twenty different bottles, including the extract of something taken out of an East Indian idol. Then he would push back his hair and stand up and pour things on the steak, at intervals of ten seconds by the watch, dabbing on little pinches of savory and smears of unguents, until you would have thought he was making up the steak for a Chinese bandit role in a Pearl Buck picture.

When he had finished making the sauce he was too depleted to eat any of it himself and had to go and lie down in the trophy room. The net effect of his labors was that of a moderately good steak covered with lots of Worcestershire.

I have a little recipe for boiled eggs which I would like to pass on to you, for I know that any readers of this page are sticklers for the art of good cooking and the even greater art of eating it:

Take the eggs, which have been boiled exactly three and a quarter minutes (they boil an extra quarter of a minute in their shells while being brought in hot water from the kitchen, making a precise total of three and a half minutes before they are opened) . Crack them with a spoon which has been warmed to the temperature of your thumb, being careful not to let little bits of egg-encrusted shell slip down the side of the cup, as this slows up the mixing, besides making rather more of a mess than you had planned. Then take a dab of butter, the size of a dab of butter, and place it perpendicularly on the upper surface of the eggs, followed by a dash of salt and a dash of pepper, performed with a left-to-right gesture.

Then plough the top surface of the egg under, until a whole new surface appears, and repeat the process of butter, salt and pepper, turning each prepared surface under and exposing a fresh one, until the whole egg content has been thoroughly mixed. Then, as a final fillip, give four sharp turns with the spoon, and wash your fingers.

And if you don't say that they are the best boiled eggs you ever ate—then maybe they aren't.

Fusillade
Near Toulon

IN GLANCING over my copy of the Paris
Matin, preparatory to studying it, I find an
interesting case of fusillade which might interest the readers of an American paper, accus-
tomed to our local dry-as-dust crime records. I
will put it down as I skim through it, and then
go over it later with a dictionary and polish it
up a bit. Following is as I understand it at first
reading:

It is from the Matin's particular correspondent at Toulon and was sent in by telephone,
no mean feat in itself over a French telephone.
It is headed: "At Brignolles a Septuagenarian
Fusillades His Family and Kills Himself."

"Three persons killed, another of whom the
state is desperate; such is the balance of a drama
of foolishness which has just come from un-
rolling itself in Brignolles.

"M. Gibion, a brasser, is proprietor of a
pretty immovable center which he found himself occupying with his wife, his three daughters and his step-father, M. Franco, age of 78

years. This last led an existence active enough, and hurled himself often to Nice, where he had interests. He was returned to this city before yesterday. On his return, he had a discussion with his kind. Since a long time, the septuagenarian, jumbled with his family, had taken his repast all alone in the kitchen.

"M. and Mme. Gibion dined with their three daughters in the dining-room, when brusquely M. Franco, who came from achieving his repast, made an irruption, armed with a revolver and a rifle. He began to play with Gibion, who led astray the cannon. The blow parted in the air. M. Gibion, infatuated, took refuge with himself on the third floor with a lodger, M. Garino. Below, the old man superciliously massacred his family."

I here draw the curtain over several details, such as the ages of the unfortunate group, and pick up the story again where the old gentleman "drew a ball of the revolver on his other granddaughter, who had vanished under the form of her mother and who was offended in the stomach.

"The criminal, who had closed himself in a neighboring chamber, lodged two balls in his head. He had enough strength left to open a

175

window and at last to precipitate himself into the street, where he settled himself, rattling."

The supreme example of understatement, which I feel justifies this rather horrid recital of carnage, is contained in the final paragraph of the story.

"One surmises," telephones the particular correspondent from Toulon, "at the flutter which provoked this tragedy at Brignolles."

Possibly now I had better get out the dictionary and make such changes in style as may be needed to get the story into tip-top shape. A word here and there may be altered, but I do hope that I am not wrong about "flutter."

Fatigue
Without Work

SOMETIME, if you want to get really tired
without doing any work yourself, just look
at the advertisements in the street-cars or in the
back of your magazine, and concentrate on the
work that has gone into every inch of each of
them. And then think: "For what?"

Do you realize that every advertisement
showing a sock, with just the words "Holeo
Socks Are Best," and every block of type reading: "We guarantee each Peak-a-Boo Drip Pan
against Burglary," has been the subject of
weeks and weeks of copy-writing, art-work, conferences, re-copy-writing, re-art-work, more
conferences, inter-office communications, conferences between the advertising agency and
the advertiser, re-copy-writing, re-art-work,
random suicides and finally the finished product, as you see it on the car-card or on the
printed page?

Does that tire you, just to think about? It is
one of the main reasons why I am tired at the
end of each day.

When you look at an advertisement for pencil-breakers, reading: "Break Your Pencils Right!" and then look carelessly away again, do you realize that you are making monkeys out of six or eight men who have staked their professional reputations, to say nothing of weeks of hard work, on that advertisement's having "dignity," "pulling-power," "consumer-appeal" and "class"? Into every layout that you so cavalierly glance at have gone at least six conferences and two broken hearts.

Let us take, for example, an advertisement for Zmart Zipper Mittens. It shows a picture of two mittens superimposed on a photograph of the Royal Poinsettia Hotel at Palm Beach. The text reads: Wherever Society foregathers, there Zmart Zipper Mittens are *"de rigueur."* That's all.

In the first place, there were lay-outs made of this. You may have thought that a pair of mittens had just been dropped on a picture of the Royal Poinsettia Hotel and then photographed. But there were conferences over whether it should be the Royal Poinsettia Hotel or an airplane view of Welfare Island; whether it should be a line-drawing or a halftone; whether one mitten should overlap the other or stand by itself with a single narcissus

178

in it. And don't think that these conferences were happy ones.

Then came the question of copy. A copy-writer submitted his first draft, which was thrown out almost before it left his hands. After a conference, he submitted another, this time using the French phrase *"de rigueur."*

And don't think that these conferences were happy ones

(Memo. from Mr. Jerfee to Mr. Berff: "It needs more class.") Two paragraphs of the second draft were thrown out, and it was decided that it would be more dignified simply to say: "Wherever Society foregathers, etc." This broke some one's heart.

Then came the question of type. Should it be set in 12-point Bodoni or 14-point Chelten-

179

ham Old Style? Should it be—Are you tired? Does it make life seem hardly worth struggling through? When you see what actually came out of all this, do you wish you had never been born?

If not, then think of the men who have to write comical captions under news photographs, like "Button up your overcoat! Here is what yesterday's snow did to Exchange street," or "Who's afraid of the big, bad Cotton Exchange? Cotton brokers celebrating the passage of the Klein-McGuiness Bill."

Think of the thousands and thousands of writers and artists being gay and light-hearted for your benefit when you never give them a tumble.

Think of me writing this piece.

Calory
Spending

I HAVE just been looking at a table showing the energy, in calories, expended per
hour by a man weighing 154 pounds under different conditions of muscular activity, and I
am shocked to find that I must come under the
designation of "Calory Hoarder." I guess that I
still must have the first calory I ever earned.

According to this table, 65 calories per hour
are expended by just sleeping and 77 by just
being awake. "Sitting at rest" uses up 100 calories per hour, making my grand total 177
calories when I am sitting at rest awake, and
165 when I am sitting at rest asleep. I can't find
any other form of muscular activity in the list
that I really go in for, certainly not by the hour.

For example, there is "reading aloud" (105),
"hand sewing" (111), "standing at attention"
(115) and "knitting" (23 stitches per minute
on sweater) which uses 116, but I don't read
aloud—or have anyone read aloud to me, if I
can help it—sew by hand, stand at attention, or
knit 23 stitches a minute on a sweater. I don't

even knit three stitches a minute on a sweater, even on a big day.

On some days, when I am in rare form and feel like stepping out, I might expend the 118 calories that are given for "dressing and undressing," but my work is such that I really don't have to get on more than a pair of slippers and a sweater to be in uniform, and it certainly doesn't take me an hour to do that, so I couldn't take credit for the full 118.

On those nights, however, when I have to put studs into a dress-shirt and button the collar, I guess that I use up enough calories to make up my quota. In fact, I note that "sawing wood" uses up 480 calories, and if sawing wood isn't easier than buttoning a 15½ collar around a 16 neck, then I'll compromise on 400 calories.

It says that singing exhausts 122 calories, but it doesn't mention humming, and that's about as far as I ever get. "Typewriting rapidly" rates 140, but I don't typewrite rapidly. In fact, there are hours when I sit at a typewriter without hitting a key.

I didn't even look to see what "ironing with a 5-pound iron" expends, for I wasn't interested. "Sweeping bare floor 38 strokes per minute" was also one of the items I didn't follow along with my finger to the calory column. In fact, "book-binding," "shoe-making," "carpentry and metal working" or "active exercise" (the latter closing at 240) seemed to me just silly to have in a column like that. What are we—living in the Middle Ages?

I was disturbed to find that "walking moderately fast" was put down at 3.75 miles per hour (300 calories). I would consider walking 3.75 miles per hour as running, and at a good fast clip at that. "Walking very fast—5.3 miles per hour" uses up the largest number of calories in the list—650—even more than running at 5.3 miles per hour (570), but we don't even have to discuss that, although I don't see how it can be. I suppose that it is because anyone foolish enough to try to run at that rate wouldn't be able to finish out the hour.

All in all, I don't suppose that, in the twenty-four hours including the 143 consumed in being asleep and being awake, I use up more than 500 calories, which is the exact amount expended in one hour of swimming, according to the table. But I don't have all that bother of changing to a swimming suit and back to street clothes again, and I don't get all wet and blue around the lips. I think I'll just spend my 500 a day, and see what happens.

Fiction
Stranger than Truth

IS TRUTH stranger than Fiction? This is a question which has half the world at loggerheads and the other half at sixes and sevens.

Of course, in order to settle it, one must know just how strange Fiction is. Then, working backward from that, we can see how strange Truth is, and come to some orderly decision satisfactory to both sides. The thing to avoid is hard feeling.

Here are a few happenings in real life which certainly are strange. If you can match them with happenings in fiction, I shall be dumbfounded.

Take, for example, the case of the man in Bermuda who was walking along the street one day recently (1756) when he stepped into a pit which had been dug by some pirates to hide a keg of gold later in the day. On crawling out, in no very good humor you may be sure, he fell forward into another pit which had been dug by some other pirates for the very same purpose. (The street was known as

"Pirate Pit Street" and was a hot-bed for buried treasures.) On pulling himself out of the second pit, in no better humor than before, he muttered to himself: "This sort of thing has got to stop." As he said this, he looked down into the first pit he had fallen into, and there he saw his own self, climbing out face to face with him! So he dropped back into the second pit and stayed there. Explanation: There were two pits.

A Philadelphia man who kept cows was one day doing his milking, and, being slightly hung over, was resting his head against the cow's side as he milked. Suddenly his ear which was pressed against the cow detected the sound of conversation being carried on in low tones. He stopped milking but kept his ear pressed tight, and was rewarded by hearing the talk change from sotto voce conversation to bitter argument, increasing in tone until he could distinguish every word. The subject of the quarrel seemed to be, as usual, a woman.

The man left his listening-post and led the cow to a butcher, and, when it had been killed and cut open, sure enough, there inside were two very small men arguing about a woman. The men were released on bail and the milkman went home, still puzzling.

Perhaps the strangest of all happenings in real life is the series of events which led a criminal to arrest himself and then escape from himself, after giving himself an ugly cut over the eye. James Gargey, of Ultimate, Pennsylvania, surprised himself in the act of tearing off steps from a house that he had just robbed.

His idea, according to a confidante of his, was to cover up his tracks and make it look like an inside job. In addition to being a clever thief, Gargey was Chief of Police of Ultimate, and, in his official capacity, was forced to arrest himself. (It was Gargey who gave W. S. Gilbert the idea for "The Mikado," for which he never got a nickel.)

Confronted by the necessity for both making an arrest and escaping, he went to a neighboring saloon (one of the saloons which did come back, in spite of the slogan "The Saloon Must Not Come Back") and treated himself to a series of concoctions invented by the bartender in an off moment when he was working on a new drink for the "Miss Pennsylvania" prize. Following these, our hero swung on himself, landing a neat left to the eye, and then, wrenching himself out of his grasp, ran pell-mell down the street and hid in a Chinese laundry until the affair had blown over. A rookie

186

policeman brought food to his superior while he was in hiding.

These little incidents in real life are, I think you will agree, as strange as anything in fiction, or, in case you think of them as fiction, as strange as anything in real life. The point is that they are pretty darned strange.

Love
Among the Thinkers

Who remembers the old days when lovers in novels used to talk about Love to each other? That was before Sociology, Biology, Communism, and the Machine Age crept into the hearts of our young people and made Thinkers of them. It used to be so that a hero who could back a heroine into a corner and fix her with a bloodshot eye, muttering: "It's the Irish eyes of you, and the crimson lips of you, and the wanton way you have of tossing the hair of you, that's driving me mad!" was pretty sure to get the rest of the way without having to change cars. But in the modern novel the hero who is not a graduate of the Rand School of Social Science and who cannot talk Values and Gestalt Psychology, while the necking is going on, might just as well resign himself to picking threads off his sleeve for the rest of his life.

Sinclair Lewis' heroines do dabble in Sex now and then (they always manage, these intellectual women, to get around to a few of the old-fashioned fundamentals somewhere during the book, and in just about the same way that their poor dear grandmothers did, too), but they constantly keep one eye on the Ratio of Biological Compromise and, at any given moment during the affair, could whip out statistics showing that Woman, as an Economic Determinant, can be expressed in terms of Thermodynamic Energy.

188

H. G. Wells' heroes, although not above an occasional affair d'amour of fairly commonplace proportions, temper their dalliance with a note of serious-minded debate on the Future of Man-As-We-Know-Him, with Special Reference to Hormones and Basal Metabolism, and, what is more, always seem able to find a young lady who will take the negative when Cupid's hour begins to drag.

It is an old story, this dialectic love-making, for Mr. Wells, for, as long ago as "Ann Veronica" he began mixing Woman's Rights with Baby Talk, but Mr. Lewis seems still fresh from what I am afraid his heroine would call the "Chem. lab." and the whole thing is to him a breathless experience in contemplative incontinence.

Let us suppose, for the purposes of this brief burlesque, that Ann Vickers meets Theodore Bulpington in the moonlight on the Day Nursery roof of the Stuyvesant Industrial Home, and that she feels the Urge to be a Woman, as even a social-worker must feel it when June brings the scent of far-off Devon wafting on the velvet waves of Night. How would they go about it?

But first we must go back to the days of their respective childhoods. (It is always necessary to begin with childhood days to show how many of the Spanish War songs and slang phrases the author remembers and to recall how funny people used to look on bicycles.)

[CHAPTER ONE]

THE strains of "On the Banks of the Wabash," as sung by three small children in high treble voices, had just died down, and the

189

first automobile in Kasawaska Center, Wisconsin, had simultaneously turned the corner of Elm and Maple Streets to the jeering cries of "Get a horse!" from the enraged citizenry.

Ann Vickers, aged three, confronted her companion, Arthur Rogers, aged five, with a determined gaze.

"Your father is a capitalist," she said.

"Capitalism is the backbone of our financial structure," replied Arthur, bridling.

"You will live to regret that statement, Arthur," said Ann. "Let me see . . . I should say in about 1933 the institution of Capitalism would be facing the greatest crisis of its career."

"Dat's a dreat bid lie," piped up little Ernest Herlinger, whose father owned the Kasawaska Light and Power Company.

"Be quiet, Ernest," responded Ann, "what do you know about Economics?"

"My father says that your father is an Anarchist," put in Arthur, thumbing his nose at Ann.

"That's the trouble with you capitalists," replied Ann, putting an all-day-sucker in her mouth, "muddy thinking. An Anarchist believes in no laws at all. My father believes in laws, but humane laws. Anarchy would get us nowhere, and I'll bet you a hundred billion trillion dollars that, by the turn of the century, some Anarchist has assassinated President Mc-Kinley."

"Let's play house," suggested little Ernest.

And, with childish cries of glee, the three tots were off for an afternoon of romping.

[CHAPTER TWO]

It had been six years since Theodore Bulpington began thinking about Religious Persecution in the Middle Ages. Theodore was now seven, and he had come to the conclusion that Religious Persecution was Sumpin Awful. Nationalism was Sumpin Awful, too. So was Cancer. The world was full of Sumpin Awfuls. This was what Theodore Bulpington decided as he lay on a cliff in Cornwall and watched the gulls swoop down on the local fishes. Gulls were Sumpin Awful, too.

But there was always Art. No matter how you felt about the Revocation of the Edict of Nantes, there was always Art, and a chap could go a long way with Aubrey Beardsley to back him up. A chap could go a long way anyway, provided he could hear Offenbach often enough and ate enough stewed fruit.

"Darwin was a mucker," said Billy Himmerdink.

"Rot!" said Theodore.

"Rot is all very well to say, but where has Evolution got us?"

"Out of the primordial ooze and slime for one thing. And very nearly into the Twentieth Century for another."

"Thanks for nothing," said Billy.

Billy was a Sumpin Awful, even though he was Theodore's cousin.

[CHAPTER THREE]

The roof of the Stuyvesant Industrial Home and Day Nursery was a silver sea in the moonlight. Theodore, standing very close behind Ann Vickers, placed one hand over hers as it rested on the parapet.

"It's funny—our meeting like this, I mean," he said.

"It's funny our not having met like this before," said Ann, without turning her head. "Woman is Man's logical mate."

"Aren't you being just a little old-fashioned?" asked Theodore.

Ann winced. "Old-fashioned" was a hard word.

"I have seen nothing in Krafft-Ebing to make me think differently," she said, laying her head ever so lightly back on his shoulder. Her hair had the odor of sweet-grass baskets.

"Since the Twelfth Century we have seen Woman come on apace," said Theodore, pressing his lips into its soft fragrance. "And yet hormones are hormones, just as ballots are ballots. You can't evade the issue by calling on Krafft-Ebing."

Ann turned so that her face was close to his.

"I have studied biology," she said, gently. "Biol. 3a and Biol. 4b in the University. It ruined my religion, but it gave me my soul."

Theodore placed his hands on either side of her face and tilted it up toward him.

"The Reformation began in 1517," he said, tenderly. "When Martin Luther drove that nail into the church door at Wittenberg, he drove it into the Heart of the World." Then he kissed her.

"You talk like a behaviorist," said Ann, as soon as she could move her lips. "Does it ever occur to you that when the machines have taken over our entire civilization, we—you and I—Man and Woman—will be left free to revert to the Pleistocene Age and just paddle about in the mud?"

"You darling!" he cried, kissing her again. "And does it ever occur to *you* that Science,

193

Literature, Religion, Invention, and Discovery, all the shibboleths of our modern civilization, are but words—words—words? Are there no such things as Values?" His arms crushed her to him. He was strong and smelled of shaving-soap.

There was a long silence, while the sound of the traffic came faintly from below.

"I've been thinking, my darling," said Ann, finally. "Didn't the Reformation begin before 1517? I mean, *really* begin?"

"You silly goose," replied Theodore, holding her at arm's length. "Of course it did. It began when the first male dinosaurus dragged himself across the glacier-swept plain toward his lady-love. It began when Cro-Magnon Man picked up Cro-Magnon Woman and carried her away to his cave. It began when Abelard ——"

"Careful!" warned Ann, smiling. "It came very near ending with Abelard, if you will remember."

And, to herself, Ann Vickers said, as she nestled closer to a tweed lapel: "Here you are, Miss Vickers, the result of centuries and centuries of progress, the fine flower of Woman-hood, possessed of the right to vote (August 26, 1920), the right to call your soul your own (September 15, 1889), and the fine instincts

194

developed by generations and generations of New England stock, and what are you doing with your hormones? You are a sport, that's what you are. Not a sport in the sense of a sporting person, but in the biological sense, as given in Webster, 'an animal or plant, or one of its parts, that exhibits sudden and spontaneous variation from the normal type.' That's what Webster thinks of you! That's what Susan B. Anthony thinks of you! That's what the God of the Israelites thinks of you! I am ashamed of you, Ann Vickers!"

While this soliloquy was going on, Theodore was pressing her closer and closer to his chest, which was not like the weak chest of Professor Dinwiddie, nor the pudgy chest of Robert Paster, nor the barrel chest of Dr. Wormser, nor any of the other chests which Ann Vickers, in her search for social justice and prison reform, had encountered as a part of her laboratory work. It was Theodore Bulpington's chest, and it was good.

At last he spoke. "I do not look for an actual revolution," he said. "Not a revolution of blood and arson, like that in France at the close of the eighteenth century. But, my darling," and he kissed her on the forehead, "the old price system must go."

She took his big, strong hand in her two little ones.

"Let's go inside," she said. "I have some good Scotch in my room . . . And it is getting chilly out here."

How
to Avoid Colds

THE prevalence of the common cold (or house-fly) at this time of year makes it advisable for everyone who possibly can to formulate a set of ten rules for their avoidance. At the end of the open season the best set of ten rules will be embroidered on a handkerchief and presented to their author to use for his own cold.

Here, as nearly as I can remember them, are my ten rules for avoiding the common head-cold:

1. Don't breathe through your mouth or your nose. These two orifices have been called "The Twin Roads to Germville" and, on a busy day, present a picture to the microscope similar to that of the Boston Turnpike. So long as people use their mouths and their noses to breathe through, we are going to have epidemics, plagues and eventual disintegration of the human race.

Your surgeon will be glad to fit you up with a small tube which can be inserted into the throat and worked with a nickel handpump. This will supply you with all the air you need for an ordinary day's breathing. Most of us get too much air anyway. Ordinary breathing air has been called "Nature's Exhaust," and the less we load ourselves up with the better.

2. Avoid crowds. This applies to all times of the year. You never know who may be in a crowd, and mingling with one may result in your being reminded of an old fifty-dollar loan or a promise to drop in and hear someone sing. Even if no one in the crowd has a cold, there is always someone who wants to push or romp, and you are pretty sure to have your hat knocked off. A good way to avoid crowds is to stay right in your room all day with the door locked.

3. Get plenty of sleep. When people come to awaken you in the morning, pull the covers up over your head and say: "Go away, I am avoiding a cold." When you have guests who hang around after midnight, excuse yourself politely by saying: "Now I will go in and get my preventive sleep. This is the season for colds, you know." If, during the afternoon, you feel drowsy at your work, just put your head over on your desk and take a little nap. Your boss will understand if you put a little sign up by

your elbow reading: "Men asleep here. Cold prevention."

4. Change heads frequently during the day. Have an extra supply of heads in your room (or in a large bag, if you travel about) and,

Excuse yourself politely

when you feel one stuffing-up, take it off and put on a fresh one.

5. Stay in a temperature of between 60 and 70 degrees. This can be done by jumping on board a train for Palm Beach and lying on the sand for a month or so. Be sure, however, to lie face up, with the arms outstretched, so that the

sun can send its actinic rays across your chest and into your eyes. This is the hardest part of this rule to follow out. The temperature of the gambling rooms will be just about right in the evening, so you won't have to lie on your back there.

6. Don't dose up with patent medicines and nostrums. A sitz-bath of rock-and-rye twice a day, using ordinary care not to bruise yourself on the rock-candy, ought to be all the medicinal treatment you will need.

7. Eat a balanced diet. No proteins, no starches, no carbohydrates. Just a good steak with lyonnaise potatoes and asparagus now and then during the day. Remember the old adage: "Stuff a cold and stuff a fever."

8. No exercise. This is all-important. Exercise just stirs up the poisons in your system and makes you a hot-bed of disease. Sit, or lie, as still as possible, and smoke constantly. If you can stand it, have somebody read aloud to you. If you can't stand it, scream, "Stop that reading out loud!"

9. If you think that you have caught a cold, call in a good doctor. Call in three good doctors and play bridge.

10. And, above all, don't catch cold.

Two
Loves

IT IS seldom that a man picks up a newspaper and, on one page alone, finds material for tender reminiscence over two early love-affairs, and yet yesterday I had exactly that experience. On one page of a rotogravure section I found photographs of both Maude Adams and Edna May.

Maude Adams came into my life first, and I think that, on the whole, my love for her was more spiritual than that which I later felt for Edna May. In fact, I may say that it was the turning point in my emotional life. I do not remember how old I was at the time, but I do know that, from then on, I put away childish things, even though I still continued the mockery of wearing short pants. What my biographers may refer to as "the Maude Adams affair" definitely marked the end of my juvenile stage.

It was in "Peter Pan" that I first saw her, but it was in "The Little Minister," and a curtain-raiser called "Hop-o'-My-Thumb" that she really got me down. I had great difficulty in breathing during "Hop-o'-My-Thumb," so great was my emotion. I went home in a daze from the theatre and refused food for two days.

Then, when I could pull myself together, I went to the Public Library and gave myself over to research among the Adamsiana in an attempt to learn all there was to know about the private life of this woman who had bewitched me. That her real name was Kiskadden and that she came from Salt Lake City were facts which, while they brought the matter slightly nearer to earth, became engraved on my heart forever. I was immensely relieved to find no reference to any marriage.

I told no one of my attachment, preferring to suffer in silence and keep my passion locked in my breast. One night I saw a young lady at a church supper who bore a slight resemblance to the woman I loved, and after mooning about in her vicinity for an hour or so finally maneuvered an introduction. As casually as I could, I asked her if she had, by any chance, ever seen "The Little Minister" or "Hop-o'-My-Thumb." (I couldn't bring myself to speak the name "Maude Adams" before strangers.) She said, "No," and asked me if they were musical comedies. I rushed from her, and never brought the matter up again to anyone. In fact, this is

the first time that I have ever brought it out
into the open, so Miss Adams herself never
knew. I wonder, now, if Fate had thrown me
in her path, if things would have been different.

My affair with Edna May was gayer. I had
gone to New York during the holidays and had

I asked her if she had ever seen "The Little Minister"

been taken to see "The School Girl" at the
Herald Square Theatre. Edna May sang a song
called "Mamie, I've a Little Canoe," and I am
frank to say that she bowled me completely off
my feet. I was fifteen at the time, so I knew
what I was about, and didn't allow myself to be
plunged into a melancholia as I had done with

Maude Adams. But when I went back to school I would hum, "Mamie, I've a Little Canoe," to my mates and, with a sly, faraway look in my eye, would let it be understood that there were facts about my trip to New York which had not come to light, but which were connected with that song and the singer of it.

I am afraid that I was something of a cad about Edna May. I understand that she later married a Mr. Lewisohn and is still living in England. I am sure that I hope she is very happy. I never was one to harbor resentment. (Mr. Lewisohn had money, I believe.)

And so I sit by my fire with this page of a rotogravure section which has stirred so many old memories in my breast. Maude Adams and Edna May! Many a man has gone further and fared worse than I. What is this—a tear coursing down my cheek? What a sentimental old fool I am, to be sure!

How
I Learned Tennis

A GREAT many people have asked me "How did you learn to play tennis?" (Maybe it was "Why *don't* you learn to play tennis?" I don't pay strict attention to everything that people ask me.) So I have decided to put down on paper the stages through which I went in order to attain the game that I play today.

"Work—work—and then more work" is the motto which everyone must adopt who has any ambition to fall down on the center court at Wimbledon. Tennis is not a game that one picks up over night, like "Truth and Consequences," or abandons overnight, like "Truth and Consequences." It is a game calling for eternal practice, constant study and easily opened pores. An extra set of arms and legs also come in handy.

My interest in tennis began when I was 4 years old, when I used to watch my brothers and sisters playing on the court just outside our house. (A short trolley-car ride to the end of the line and then by buckboard through virgin forest to the Tennis Club.) I used to stand by the sidelines and help them by running out into the court whenever a ball was served. Sometimes I even succeeded in actually intercepting a serve before it hit the ground, but always managed to be on the spot when it was returned.

"That kid will play tennis some day," said one of my brothers, proudly, "either that, or end in the electric chair." The popular vote, at that time, was for the electric chair.

Then came the day when I was given my first racket. It was my sister's racket, and I was given it across the neck and shoulders, but there wasn't a prouder little boy in town that day. I had won (for my sister's opponent) the Ladies' Singles Championship of the Worcester Country Club.

Then I began the practice for myself. I got an old ball (all tennis balls are old balls) and a racket, and would get up at six every morning and bat the ball against the side of the house where our guest-room was. This took perseverance and stamina, as complaints began to pour in and my ball and racket were locked up in my parents' room until ten a. m. But I overcame this obstacle by riding my bicycle back and forth at 6 a. m. and ringing the bell constantly. You see, I was a determined little cuss.

When I went away to school, each boy had to choose one form of athletic sport and indulge in it every day between the hours of two and four p. m. I chose tennis, as the courts were quite a

Riding my bicycle back and forth at 6 A. M.

distance from the school buildings and, as they were always full, I could sometimes get in a whole two hours' sleep under the trees without being reported. And I may say, incidentally, that all during my tennis career I have always found the courts full enough to justify a little snooze now and then, or even a trip to a neighboring town for a movie.

As my form gradually improved to the point where I did not rely entirely on the lob for returning the ball, I developed a system which has been the backbone of my game, both in

*I found that what I was doing naturally was making
my opponent practically helpless*

tournament play and random rallying. The idea back of it is to get your opponent to laughing so hard that he is unable either to serve or get the ball back. (A good-natured opponent is almost a necessity in this form of play.)

This I do by making comical faces, striking grotesque poses, and falling down occasionally with a loud clatter. This trick (for I suppose it is a trick, really) came to me accidentally, when I found that what I was doing naturally was making my opponent practically helpless in my hands. He sometimes would even give me the game by default and retire to the side-lines in hysteria.

So I cultivated this knack of mine, and to it I lay what success I have had in the game to date. Naturally, I prefer singles to doubles, as a partner does not always think it so funny.

Then, about seven years ago, I had the good fortune to throw my left knee badly out of joint at a wedding, with the result that practically any physical exertion on my part now results in its bending backward as well as forward. So, while other people are lashing themselves into a lather at tennis, I can sit under the trees and knit, with the excuse, "My old knee, you know. Darn it!" Thus I have acquired an outlook on the game which few professionals have, which, after all, is my only justification for these few notes.

Old Suits
For New

THE time is drawing near for my semi-annual humiliation before the clothing trade. When I go in to buy a new suit I must, according to an ancient blue-law which still survives, be wearing something. And, in my case, it is always an old blue suit.

Now, tailors hate old blue suits. They practically spit on them. Even if the suit came originally from them, they don't like it. If it has another tailor's name in it, it is all they can do to bring themselves to speak to you. And all my old suits are not only blue, but all came from different places.

I never got around to that well-ordered system of living where one always buys suits in the same place. I buy a new suit on the corner of the street where my old one begins to fall apart.

Sometimes, if I can stand still long enough without screaming, I have it made to order. Otherwise, I just go in somewhere and say: "A blue suit, please. Just send it!" and rush out.

This gives one a bad name among the better class of tailors.

On whatever day I finally bring myself to enter a tailor's shop to be fitted for a new suit, I always seem to have on a model that I bought once in Augusta, Me., while on a fishing trip. It says "Pine Tree State Outfitters" inside the pocket. I keep thinking that I have thrown that suit away, but it always turns out to be on me when I go into a clothing store or a tailor's for a new rig. And the tailor thinks less than I do of it.

I begin taking the coat off before I am in the shop, and hide it under my arm so that he won't see the label. But sooner or later, he spots it and the jig is up. From then on I have a hard time convincing him that I am not in the market for dungarees.

I once set fire to my dinner-clothes when I was in Rome and had to have a new set made. The man who recommended me to his tailor said: "Be sure to tell him that I sent you. He is very fussy about whom he makes clothes for. He refused to make a suit for a well-known movie actor once because he didn't like the Hollywood cut of the suit he was wearing."

This did nothing to reassure me, but I had

211

Sooner or later, he spots it

to have the suit and knew of no other place to go.

On visiting the tailoring establishment of the great man, I found that he didn't speak English and thought that I was a button salesman. An accomplished assistant, however, translated to him that Mr. Doaks had sent me, and he asked me to step into his private office. As I crossed the threshold I realized that I had on a ready-made suit which I had bought in Hollywood! The skylight was too high up for me to jump through, and the door was already closed behind me.

The maestro looked me up and down, and made some crack to his assistant in Italian. The assistant laughed a nasty laugh, and told me to take off my coat. Although it is customary to take off one's coat while being measured for a suit, I had somehow hoped that I could avoid it this time. I thought some of saying that all I wanted was the trousers, but he wouldn't have liked that, I was sure.

So I took my coat off and doubled it up quickly, and tried to shove it casually under a bolt of cloth on the table. Then followed a series of quick maneuvers on the part of the assistant and me, he trying to get a look at the label, I fighting my heart out to prevent him.

While I was being measured he took a peek, and then came out with another crack in Italian which sent his master into stitches and threw me into a state of furious blushing. I kept hearing the name of the friend who had sent me introduced into the badinage, and gathered that they thought he had been playing some sort of joke on them. So, as a joke, they went through with the horrid business, and I got my dinner clothes.

I still have that suit, and I think that when I go to get my new blue suit this Spring I will wear it to the tailor's. At any rate, he can't sneer at the label.

Bobbing for Words

AFTER eight months of snooping about New England getting natives to talk, the American Council of Learned Societies or Something has completed a ten-thousand-page report as the first section of "A Linguistic Atlas of the United States and Canada," in which they show that in eastern Massachusetts an apple dumpling is called "pan dowdy" and that on Block Island a seesaw is known as a "tipity-bounce." Now, in order to finish their report, all that they have to do is canvass the rest of the United States and Canada. It looks like the end of the unemployment crisis, boys!

We can save the Learned Societies a lot of lunch money for their field-workers in the New York district by outlining for them some of the linguistic *bibelots* which have been handed down from generation to generation (except when one generation wouldn't accept them) and have finally become a part of our local speech, otherwise known as the Litvokshire dialect. This is a combination of practically every language except that used by the common magpie or shrike, together with certain of the simpler movements of the Language of the Fan. (Three waves of closed fan up and one down: "I love you;" one down stroke with half-open fan: "Your cigarette is burning me!" etc. etc.)

For example, a paper-clip used to clean out a pipe when no pipe-cleaner is handy is generally known as "a paper-clip used in lieu of pipe-cleaner." But in northern New York City and as far south as Eighty-sixth Street it is called a "gleenip," in the midtown sections a "glip," and in some districts of lower Manhattan a "glower-dip." The use of "glower-dip" in this connection is particularly uninteresting as it shows the influence of the old Dutch settlers who lived in the region, some of whom are still buried in the neighborhood of what is now Broad Street, which accounts for what activity there is in that district. These old Dutch settlers (they probably weren't *old* Dutch settlers when they settled there, but they certainly are old now, and don't think that they don't know it) had a word for the cream which comes off milk-bottle caps onto the table. They called it "globber-dip." The resemblance between this and "glower-dip" is startling, but the connection between bits of cream and a paper-clip is not so easy to work out. We are still investigating this.

In most sections of the country a fox is known simply as a "fox" (*pl.* "foxes"). In certain sections of Long Island, however, it is called a "fuchsia," although many of the natives who use the word "fuchsia" insist that they mean by it a certain type of evening primrose which grows in their gardens. Our investigators have tried to tell them that the name of the flower is *"fuchsia gracilis"* or "root-rash," and that when they use the word "fuchsia" they mean "fox," but the natives are adamant. "It's a flower," they keep saying over and over again, which makes it very difficult for us to get on with our research work. They *must* mean "fox" by it, for all through this section we find the influence of the carpetbaggers from the South who came up after the Civil War to try and establish a political dynasty of white folks. This element, in an attempt to be super-refined in their speech, tortured the plural of "fox" into "feex," feeling that "foxes" must be wrong, or at any rate an approximation of baby-talk "foxies." Nowadays, one very seldom hears, even on Long Island, that three "feex" came into a chicken yard and stole the chicken wire, but the influence is still there and it is almost certain that when natives of this region say "fuchsia" they mean "fox," because that is what we set out to prove.

Many interesting variations in the pronunciation of vowels and certain consonants in different sections of New York can be explained by the use of chewing-gum or the affected habit of holding the tongue between the teeth while speaking to give the impression of indifference and sophistication. Thus we find the residents of the eastern sections pronouncing "o" as if it were "oth," as in the word "other," while to the south we find the "g" sound corrupted to a strange combination of "l" and "w." (No examples are handy at the moment, but our reports are not all in.) In the neighborhood of Fifty-second Street, and as far north as Sixtieth, where the speakeasy influence has crept in, vowels and consonants are used interchangeably and whole syllables are lopped off simply to make the going easier. Thus we find "absulith" for "absolutely," "inbulibtily" for "indubitably," and nothing at all for "hyperaesthesia."

These few gleanings from our own field-workers' reports may be of some service to the American Council of Learned Societies in their work of compiling a Linguistic Atlas of the United States and Canada. If, however, they *are* used, we shall expect a cut on the sales of the book.

A Few Figures for Unproductive Labor

I THINK that if I had it all to do over again (and it looks now as if it wouldn't be a bad idea) , I would go in more for manual labor. In times of economic crises like this, it is the manual laborer who gets the pick of the statistics.

In unemployment relief, for example, the statisticians figure out that an appropriation of ten million dollars to build a roadway across the Gulf of Mexico would give employment to two million men. Two million men who can build roadways across gulfs, that means.

All plans for a new economic order are drawn up in terms of the number of men it will take to tan hides in fifteen minutes, or construct dams in four days, or open oysters in a year. Hide-tanners, dam-builders, and oyster-openers are going to be sitting pretty in the Golden Age. But no one has a plan for those of us who just copy figures from one book to another, or draw borders for photographic layouts, or poke at the letter "x" on typewriters all day. No new order is arranged for us; no appropriations are made

I would go in more for manual labor

for us; we aren't even included in a percentage bracket in statistics. We haven't got a statistic among us.

It is this lack of statistical importance that hurts. If only somebody would call us 79 per cent of something. In lieu of a more detailed study of the subject of "Nonproductive Typewriting: Its History and Economic Significance," I submit some figures herewith which may console at least a portion of the citizenry for whom no state roads are being built.

For the past two thousand years (that is, up until the invention of the typewriter by Elias Howe, who invented the sewing machine really, and who lived to regret it when he found that the French were calling it a *machine à coudre*) , Mankind drifted along on the theory that anyone who could work a quill pen without poking himself in the eye with the feather end was a writer. But even then the grim spectre of the Machine was hovering in the distance (1850 or 1860) .

With the invention of Elias Howe by the typewriter (or sewing machine) , the tide turned, the tide which was to engulf us all in its maw. (It has been definitely proven that a tide *has* a maw, so don't write in.)

The first typewriters were crude things, necessitating a ground crew to work them like a reaper (also invented by Elias Howe in 1850 or 1860), one man to ride back and forth on the carriage and ring the bell at the end of the line, another to lurch into the keys to make them strike, and still a third to feed the paper into the holder. But, ungainly as it was, Elias Howes' "Black Bertha" was the forerunner of the Modern Age which was eventually to crowd the writer to the wall. For it introduced Energy into the picture.

From then on, writers began to have to hit typewriter keys right and left, tug at ribbons and then get up and wash their hands, monkey with hidden springs in the back of the machine without even seeing what they were doing, and in other ways to dissipate that God-given lethargy which should have been going into the avoidance of creative work. This state of affairs brought on the French Revolution (Elias Howe, 1859-1860).

STATISTICS

(Merely glance through this)

In 1904 it took 1,487 man-hours to produce 1905, which, in turn, required 3,856 man-hours to hold its own. This made 3,000,000 foot-pounds of energy (a foot-pound being the number of feet in a pound). This is, of course, all *per capita.* In 1907 the United Kingdom, or 5,-687 feet-pounds per second per second (in 1905, that is), with an area of 4,786 square miles or 5,000 foot-men per man-pounds. This gives us 2,586,950 or 4,967,498 or 4,687 (or even just 4) thermal units, with 56 per cent of a population of 354,000,000. (My, what a big country!) This does *not* include cost of production.

PROOF

The *phenomena* involved in the *functional operation* of a *social mechanism* are *constant,* and, at the same time, *variable.*

Science is the methodology of the determination of the most probable. This means that the postulate that *energy determinants* which are *variable* to each other and *variable to themselves,* thereby nullifying the whole goddamned thing.

PROOF

If a writer can turn out 600 foot-pounds of copy per foot-pound day, and, through the introduction of the sewing machine, can increase his output by 580 per cent, the result will be that, within 25 years (twenty-five years), he will be reduced to writing letters to himself to keep up his output. And, as most professional writers are very bad letter-writers (especially those who write letters with an eye to having them bound up some day for the Christmas trade), it will soon be so that writers are so sick of their own stuff that they can't bring themselves even to read proof on what they have written without pitting up. I have a hard enough time as it is just reading back over what I have written.

But I do hope that, with these few figures and this short scientific analysis of the future, I have in some way compensated the writing craft for a continued neglect on the part of the statisticians which can be considered only as having been deliberate and personal.

Those
Frescos

I T HAS been said that every great work of art has a story behind it, if we only know where to look. This is obviously untrue.

However, it is not generally known that Michaelangelo never really painted the frescos in the Sistine Chapel in Rome. They were done by a man named Harris. I do not make this statement on my own authority, but on the authority of Mr. Harris himself. He is right here in the room with me as I write—and has been drinking.

It seems that Harris (who must be quite an old man by now, although he looks about thirty-five) was in Rome at the time when Pope Julius the second commissioned Michaelangelo to paint something on the ceiling of the chapel. "Something—*anything*" was the way the orders read. Harris, who was studying art at the time, heard about it and figured out that it was his dish, Michaelangelo or no Michaelangelo.

As Harris very well knew, Michaelangelo didn't really want to do the frescos, as he was by

226

trade a sculptor and felt that painting was beneath him. (The fact that this painting was to be done on a ceiling made no difference.) So, as he and Harris were sitting around kidding one evening, Michaelangelo said, "Friend Harris, how about a little ghost-painting for me?" Harris said nothing at the time, not speaking Italian.

Well, it turned out that what Michaelangelo wanted was somebody to do the job for him and sign his name to it, as he was busy on a piece of sculpture at the time and had got it all finished but the hips and didn't want to drop it. You can understand how he felt. I know that *I* can and Harris could. (I have just checked up on this point.)

So the next day Harris put on a beard like Michaelangelo's and climbed up on the scaffold with his paints. Michaelangelo shaved off his beard to look like Harris (quite a test of friendship, if you could see Harris) and went back to work on his sculpture. So everything was hunkey-dory.

Well, as Harris puts it, he soon found out that he had bitten off more than he could chew. For four years he lay on his back on that scaffold, painting and rubbing out, painting and rubbing out, until he almost died. "I never was so cramped in all my life," he told me. And I can believe him.

People kept coming in and looking up at him, but, as all they could see was his back and little fringes of his beard, they thought that it was Michaelangelo sure enough, and as the stuff seemed to be coming along all right, nobody ever questioned him. Raphael, whose friends had induced the Pope to give Michaelangelo the job, hoping that he would show himself up, kept popping in and out and was furious at the way things were going. There isn't anything bad enough that Harris can say about Raphael.

Four years is a long time to lie on your back and paint on a ceiling. When he finally got down, leaving the whole thing unfinished because his back hurt so, he changed beards with Michaelangelo and went back to his own studio. "I'm frankly fed up!" he said. "Finish it yourself. Friendship is one thing—arthritis is another!"

And Michaelangelo, who really was a swell guy (according to Harris) , said "O. K. Harris! Let it go!" So they let it go, and that is why the frescos were never finished. You can go and look for yourself if you don't believe it.

Now Harris tells me that he wishes I wouldn't print the story, as it might get him in wrong with his fellow artists. But I think that the whole thing might as well be brought out now as later in some scandalous book of memoirs. Harris has his living to make, and I can't go on supporting him forever.

The Soothsayer

IF BY any chance, you have any old diaries of yours lying around in a box, take my advice and don't start browsing through them. It is hard enough to keep one's chin up these days without digging back into the past to make a monkey of one's self.

I kept a diary from 1904 to 1921, more out of nervousness than anything else, and I give you my word a less important record has never been compiled. It would seem impossible to write over six thousand pages, covering some of the world's most momentous years, and still not have a single one worth reading, and yet I accomplished this herculean task. Even I was bored reading through them, so you can imagine how an outsider would take it.

On those pages where I was not being dull, I was being embarrassing. Almost any personal opinion set down in a diary reads like an extract from a high-school essay in ten years, but I outdid myself in immaturity. Aside from the language, which was of the early Penrod school, the opinions themselves were fatuous to the point of being almost pathological. I wasn't right once in seventeen years.

As no one else is ever going to get a look at these diaries so long as I have a bullet in my rifle, I will summarize for posterity my prognostications and meditations on world affairs, just to show how little a college education can do for a boy and, if possible, to keep future generations from committing themselves on paper. Following are some of the main points on which I allowed myself to give opinions:

As late as August 1st, 1914, I was adamant in my belief that there would be no war. My point (and I haven't the slightest inkling today of what went on in my mind when I made it) was that Wall Street would not permit it! Even without the written evidence of my diary, I went on record to this effect in a series of long talks given to my family during those nightmare days, in which scoffing at the very idea of war was the mildest of my methods.

Unfortunately I had to shout these opinions, as I was reassuring a deaf aunt, who had a daughter living in Paris at the time. "Don't you worry!" I yelled in her ear, in tones that rang up and down the coast of Maine. "There'll be no war!" And then I repeated my mysterious refrain, culled from some twisted corner of my brain: "Wall Street won't permit it!" As it turned out, I was wrong.

Once the war was on, however, I accepted my defeat good-naturedly and laughingly gave it six weeks. "Germany has put her foot in it,"

"Don't you worry!" I yelled in her ear

was my phrasing of the international situation, and, when England went in, I almost gave up reading papers, so sure was I that the thing was as good as over. I told my aunt this, too, and she stopped worrying.

We can pass over my tactical predictions in the conduct of the war with a lump generalization: "One hundred per cent wrong." America would not go into the thing. Wilson wouldn't permit it. (I had dropped Wall Street by this time.) America would send an armada of airplanes in a non-stop flight across the Atlantic which would end the war in two days.

I was convinced that National Prohibition would never become a part of the Constitution (somebody, I've forgotten who, wouldn't permit it), and, as short a time ago as January of last year, I gave it as my opinion that workers for Repeal were a lot of crack-brained visionaries.

"We in New York think that Prohibition is unpopular because we are in the center of anti-Prohibition sentiment. Wait until the Middle West is heard from! The Middle West will never permit Repeal! The Eighteenth Amendment may be modified but no one living today will ever see it out of the Constitution!"

Returning from Germany a year ago last December, I smiled knowingly at the then current apprehension over Hitler's growing power. I happened to know, from private conversations with certain parties high in Berlin diplomatic circles, that the whole thing was a trick to let Hitler have a certain amount of power and then wait for him to hang himself with it. The

233

hanging process would take just about six weeks, according to my reckoning.

With this record of prognostication behind me, I see no reason why I shouldn't team up with H. G. Wells on a book to be called "The World Tomorrow: A Glimpse into the Future." My luck has got to turn sometime. A man can't go on being wrong all his life. Or maybe I don't know my own strength.

Life
Begins at (fill in space)

YOU, men of 40, and you women of 39 who are really 40—what's all this I hear about your being middle-aged? Why, you're just kids —slightly obese kids—that's all! Don't you realize that you are "standing with reluctant feet" (glasses will correct all that) on the brink of Life's Great Adventure—Hardening of the Arteries?

You are practically only one stage beyond Puberty. First there is Babyhood, then Childhood, then Puberty, then 40-to-45. Sometimes Puberty even comes after 40-to-45, and then is when the boy or girl is cutest. Gangling and gawky, but lovable. You could just take them up in your arms and throw them into the lake.

You think that just because you gasp for breath when you lean over to fasten your skates, you are no good any longer. Poppycock! Life is just beginning for you, if you only knew it— and if Life only knew it.

Just think of all the things you can do after 40! Professor Webster was 57 when he cut up

Dr. Parkman and threw him into the furnace of the Harvard Medical School, and Dr. Parkman was 70 himself! Nero was 52 when he set fire to Rome. Thomas Jukes was 54 when he married his own daughter to conceal the fact that he had killed her first husband. And, I myself, was 42 when I fell down a flight of steps and got water on the knee. Middle-age? Bosh!

In the old days there was perhaps some reason for growing old after 40, or possibly for not even reaching 40 at all. The Indians did a great deal toward making a man feel unfit at an early age. If you had to spend the day hewing through great trees and great bowls of corn-meal mush with a coon-skin cap on, and then found yourself in the evening having to look around all over the house for your scalp, there might be some excuse for your saying: "I'm all in, Bessie! I guess I must be getting old."

Then, if you lived later in our country's history, and had to pedal all over hell-and-gone on one of those high bicycles, or dance those hop-skip-and-a-jump waltzes to "The Beautiful Blue Danube," or invent a steamboat, or do any of the thousand things our grandfathers had to do to keep the country going in its infancy, then 40 was old, especially as college boys of 19 wore enough whiskers and eyebrows for a man of 70.

But today, with no business to rush us and no need for taking any more exercise than is involved in getting in and out of taxis (getting out is the hardest), why should we run down? A man of 40 today has nothing to worry him but falling hair, inability to button the top button, failing vision, shortness of breath, a tendency of the collar to shut off all breathing, trembling of the kidneys to the tempo of whatever tune the orchestra is playing, and a general sensation of giddiness when the matter of rent is brought up. Today, 40 is Life's Golden Age.

So, it's heads up—Shoulders back! Stomachs in or, at any rate, up a little! And it's one, two —one, two-one, two—the boys of the Over-Forty Brigade!

Only we must all remember not to try running more than a block for a train.

Yesterday's
Sweetmeats

IT IS a rather dangerous thing to note encouraging tendencies in our national life, for just as soon as some one comes out with a statement that we are better than we used to be, we suddenly prance into another war, or a million people rush out and buy Crude Oil, preferred, or there is an epidemic of mother murders, and we are right back in the neolithic age again with our hair in our eyes.

But in the matter of children's candy I am afraid that we shall have to come right out and say definitely that the trend is upward. When I look back on the days of my youth and remember the candy that I used to impose on my stomach, the wonder is that I ever grew up to be the fine figure of a man that I now am. The wonder is that I ever grew up at all. Perhaps that was the idea, and I fooled them.

There were two distinct brands of candy in my day: the candy you bought in the drug store on Sunday, when the candy shops were closed, and the week-day, or Colored Corrosion,

brand, which, according to all present-day
standards of pure food, should have set up a
bright green fermentation, with electric lights,
in the epiglottises of nine-tenths of the youth
of that time.

The wonder is that I ever grew up

We can dismiss the Sunday drug-store candy
with a word, for it was bought only once a week
and then only for lack of something better. Its
flavor was not enhanced by the fact that it was
kept in tall glass jars, like appendixes, down at
the end of the store where the prescriptions
were filled, and consequently always had a faint

suspicion of spirits of niter and sod. bicarb. about it.

The delicacy called "colt's foot," for instance, which came in long ridged sticks, to be sucked with little or no relish, not only tasted of old French coffee on the second or third brewing, but gave you the undesirable feeling that it was also good for sore throat. The Sunday licorice sticks were larger and more unwieldy, and were definitely bitter on the tongue, besides costing a nickel apiece. Although the rock candy was sweet, it lacked any vestige of imagination in its make-up and made the eating of candy a hollow mockery, and, of course, horehound was frankly medicinal and could be employed only when everything else had failed.

It was on week days that the real orgy of poisoned and delicious candy took place, a dissipation which was to make a nation of dyspeptics of the present generation of business men and political leaders. This candy was usually bought in a little store run by an old lady (probably an agent in the employ of the German government, in a far-sighted scheme to unfit the American people for participation in the war which was to come), and your arrival was heralded by the jangle of a little bell not very cleverly concealed on the top of the door. This was followed by a long period of concentration, the prospective customer sliding his nose along the glass case from end to end, pausing only to ask the price of particularly attractive samples. The smell of those little candy shops is probably now a vanished scent of a bygone day, for it combined not only the aroma of old candies and leather baseballs, but somehow the jangle of the little bell entered into one's nostrils and titillated two senses at once.

In this collection of tasty morsels the one which haunts my memory most insistently is a confection called the "wine cup," a cone-shaped bit of colored sugar filled with some villainous fluid which, when bitten, ran down over the chin and on to the necktie. It was capped by a dingy piece of marshmallow which was supposed to be removed with the teeth before drinking the ambrosia within, but usually at the first nibble the whole structure collapsed, with the result that inveterate "wine-cup" consumers had a telltale coating of sugared water down the front of the coat, and, on a cold day, a slight glaze of ice on the chin. What went on in the stomach no one knows, but it does not make a very pretty picture for the imagination.

This was followed by a long period of concentration

Another novelty was an imitation fried egg in a small frying pan, the whole sticky mess to be dug out with a little tin spoon which always bent double at the first application and had to be thrown away. The procedure from then on was to extract the so-called "egg" with the teeth, with the chin jammed firmly into the lower part of the "frying pan" as a fulcrum. This, too, left its mark on the habitué, the smear sometimes extending as high up as the forehead if the nose was very small, as it usually was.

There was one invention which was fortunately short-lived, for even in those days of killers' candy it was a little too horrible for extended consumption. It consisted of two cubes (the forerunner of our bouillon cubes of today) which, on being placed each in a glass of water and mixed with a soda-fountain technique, proceeded to effervesce with an ominous activity and form what was known either as "root beer," "ginger ale," or "strawberry soda," according to the color of the cubes.

The excitement of mixing them was hardly worth the distinct feeling of suicide which accompanied the drinking of the result, for God knows what they were or what the chemical formula for the precipitate could have been. Probably something which could have gone into the manufacture of a good, stable house paint or even guncotton.

The little mottoes, in the shape of tiny hearts, which carried such varied sentiments as "I Love You," "Skiddoo," "Kick Me," and "Kiss Me Quick," were probably harmless enough in their make-up, although I would always mistrust anything colored pink, but transporting them from shop to school and around the town loose in the pocket soon rendered them grimy and covered with gnirs, and unfit for anything involving an æsthetic sense.

"Nigger babies" also made poor pocket candies, especially when in contact with "jelly beans." (The "jelly bean" seems to have survived down the ages and still is served in little bean pots from the original stock in the store. It would be interesting to discover why.) Licorice whips and "all-day suckers" (which changed color and design on being held in the mouth, a fact which seemed miraculous at the time, but which, on contemplation, sends a slight shudder down the middle-aged spine) were probably the safest of all early twentieth-century candies, but even they would probably fail miserably to pass the test of the Bureau of Standards at Washington.

Worst of all was the "prize package," a cone

244

of old newspaper containing the odds and ends of the day's refuse—hard marshmallows with enough thumbprints on them to convict the candy dealer ten times over, quantities of tired pop corn which had originally been pink, strange little oddments of green and red sugar which, even in their heyday, could not have been much, and, as the Prize, either a little piece of tin in the approximate shape of a horse or a button reading "Bust the Trusts." My gambling instinct made these "prize packages" a great favorite for my pennies, and it is to these and to old Mrs. Hill, who ran the candy shop and dispensed her largesse in this great-hearted manner, that I lay my present inability to eat eggs which have been boiled for more than eight seconds. Dear, *dear* Mrs. Hill!

And so, regardless of the present generation's freedom and reputed wildness, I will take a chance on their stomachs being in better shape at forty than mine is, for bootleg alcohol, whatever its drawbacks, takes away that craving for sweets which was the ruin of my generation.

Latest
Ghost Reports

THE folk-lore of many countries abounds in ghost-stories (e. g. the story of John Smith and Pocahontas and the Framing of the Constitution in our own land) , but it is seldom that modern history brings to light such an eerie account as that which comes to us over the wires from Irgendflaschungenden, Bavaria. It almost discredits disbelief.

According to reliable information, here is what has happened: On August 3rd, a peasant named Karl Klatsch was walking home from the village of Ober-Irgenflaschungenden to the silo in which he lived, when, in the middle of the moon-lit road, he was confronted by an apparition.

"Ein Gespenst!" he cried, translating it immediately into "A ghost!" for his English hearers.

(Herr Klatsch had not had a drink since Prohibition went into effect in Germany.)

The sight that he saw was startling in the extreme. Straight ahead of him, half in a tree

246

"Ein Gespenst!" he cried

and half in the sky, was the shadow of an enormous man. It wasn't really so much the shadow of a man as it was the shadow of a weasel, but it did have arms and legs and a man's body and head. The expression was more that of a weasel. The expression and the general bearing. But let Herr Klatsch tell in his own words: (He speaks with a Bavarian dialect) :

"I' ha'ein groas' Mensch geseh' oohn' Gesisht und oohn' Fingernaagle, und da' hab I geschrie und doamit weo geloafen soa schnell wie moaglish." (*Herr Klatsch also has a kleft palate.*)

Face to face with such a spectre, the peasant was in a quandary. Should he drop dead right there or run a few feet first? With that cagey, quick-thinking for which all Bavarians are noted, he decided to run as far as he could before dropping dead. When last seen he was just clearing the last of the Harz Mountains.

The next night the same apparition was seen by three more peasants in a field where they were engaged in catching little horses. All three saw it and all three gave up catching little horses for the fun of being the first to tell of their adventure in the town.

The town was soon in an uproar and the Burgermeister appointed a commission to go out into the field and make notes. "It is probably an optical illusion," said the Burgermeister, who was tied up with town matters that night and could not get away.

The commission went as far as the outskirts of the town, where they held a meeting and decided that the Burgermeister was probably right, as he had been right about everything since he took over the office, except possibly filling the reservoir with frogs to eat the mosquito-eggs. So they made up a report saying that, in their opinion, it was distinctly an optical illusion, and then adjourned until Fall.

But the townspeople themselves were not satisfied, especially as thirteen or fourteen more of them saw the strange, gigantic figure on three successive nights and it finally got to such a state that large picnic parties were arranged to go out in buses and watch the Thing as it roamed back and forth against the sky and among the trees, making weird noises like a horse whinneying. They never got closer to it than a mile and a half, but that was close enough for anything they might want to do with it.

At last the news of the Irgendflaschungenden ghost reached Munich, where, by a coincidence, there was a conference of ghost-experts in session. A plane was immediately chartered, and then abandoned in favor of the railway, and a delegation of the best specialists in Germany rushed to the little Bavarian town, which was now the center of attention in that district. At last the mystery was about to be solved.

The odd part of the whole thing is that it turned out really to be a ghost, and is still there.

Dogs
and Public Service

THE meter-readers and collectors for the Consolidated Gas Company of New York City do not seem to have quite caught the knack of making friends with dogs. During the past year 198 of them were badly enough bitten to require medical attention. This sort of thing obviously couldn't go on, even from the dogs' point of view.

So the company has issued a book of instructions to its 20,000 employes. It is called "Dogs: How to Approach and Handle Them," and, according to Time, it contains the following rules:

1. Make a little noise, to let the dog know that you are coming.
2. Show no alarm at growls or barks. They are simply challenges.
3. Welcome the dog's acquaintance-making sniffs.
4. Make no sudden or unnatural movements.
5. Speak only in a confident, friendly voice.
6. Keep your hands off.
7. Impress the dog with the propriety of your visit.

These rules sound simple, but I should think that one or two of them would call for quite a bit of finesse. The last one, Rule No. 7, for example. How would you go about impressing a dog with the propriety of your visit?

My instinct would be to say to the dog, "in a confident, friendly voice" (Rule No. 5) : "Come on over here on the steps a minute, old boy. I want to talk to you." Then, when you and he were comfortably seated, you could point out to him that every age and every country has had varying standards of what is proper and what isn't proper.

"Propriety is a question of environment" you could tell him, "and it is only a very narrow-minded person who tries to impose his standards of propriety on others. And you don't want to be thought narrow-minded, do you, Werewolf?"

And he would probably shake his head, possibly with his teeth still in the calf of your leg.

Then you could show him that, under our present economic system (which is already undergoing radical changes) it is necessary for public service corporations to make collections and make repairs, and that, so long as we live under this system (a bad one, you agree) , people like you must, of necessity, make periodic calls.

"You see that, don't you, old fellow?" you could ask, just before you faint. And, if he is any kind of dog at all he will be impressed with the propriety of your visit and let go.

Just what "little noise" could be made to let the dog know that you are coming (Rule No.

Skipping and singing, "I'm coming, I'm coming!"

1) is another problem. You might begin skipping and singing, "I'm coming, I'm coming!" just as you get to the gate, or perhaps carry a zither with you and strum a few chords softly in the middle distance. Another good way would be to hide behind the gatepost and call out:

"Guess who's here! Gassy-mansy!" and then appear slowly, waggling a finger coyly.

On second thought, perhaps that wouldn't be so good. It might come under the head of "unnatural movements," which are warned against in Rule No. 4. The business of welcoming the dog's "acquaintance-making sniffs" and speaking in "a confident, friendly voice" is all very well, and goes hand in hand with "showing no alarm at growls or barks." These are the tactics that I invariably adopt, but I sometimes wonder if they fool the dog. My cheery "How are ya, boy?" spoken much too loudly and with a great deal too much confidence, has often failed to impress even me, especially if the dog keeps on growling.

Dogs are no fools, and I have a feeling that they recognize the sham and have contempt for it. I think that it might be better just to shut your eyes and walk right by, without any "How are ya, boy?" at all. Then at least, you would be keeping your self-respect, if not the cuff to your trouser leg.

It is a difficult problem that the Gas Company faces, and an even more difficult one that its employes face. Why couldn't householders just be taught to make their own repairs, and have the company let the unpaid bills ride?

Johnny-
on-the-Spot

I F YOU want to get a good perspective on history in the making, just skim through a collection of news-photographs which have been snapped at those very moments when cataclysmic events were taking place throughout the world. In almost every picture you can discover one guy in a derby hat who is looking in exactly the opposite direction from the excitement, totally oblivious to the fact that the world is shaking beneath his feet. That would be me, or at any rate, my agent in that particular part of the world in which the event is taking place.

I have not seen an actual photograph of the shooting of the Austrian Archduke at Serajevo, but I would be willing to bet, if one is in existence, that you could find, somewhere off in the right foreground, a man in a Serbian derby looking anxiously up the street for a trolley car. And probably right up in the foreground a youth smiling and waving into the camera.

Revolutionary disturbances are particularly subject to this blasé treatment on the part of by-standers. Photographs which have come up from Cuba lately, and even those of the wildest days in Russia during the Reign of Terror— photographs taken at the risk of the lives of the photographers themselves—all show, some-where in their composition, an area of complete calm in which at least one man is looking at his watch or picking his teeth.

In one which I have before me from Havana we see crowds of people fleeing before machine gun bullets, soldiers dashing hither and yon with uplifted sabres, puffs of smoke stippling the background, and down in one corner, by a news kiosk, a man in his shirtsleeves looking up at a clock.

At any rate, there'll be one guy who knows what time the trouble started—provided he knew that it *had* started.

Are these men in derby hats really men of iron, who take revolutions and assassinations in their stride as all part of the day's work, or are they hard of hearing, or near-sighted, or, possi-bly, are they just men who go through life missing things?

I like to think of them as in the third cate-gory, for I know that if I were on the spot during any important historical event I would not know about it until I read the papers the next day. I am unobservant to the point of being what scientists might call "half-witted." It isn't that I don't see things, but that I don't register them. This is what makes it so difficult for me in traffic.

I could have worked in a shop in the Place de la Bastille, or have sold papers across from the Old State House in Boston, or have been an usher in Ford's Theatre in Washington, and yet would probably have noticed nothing of the events for which those spots are famous. I possibly might have been aware of a slight commotion and, if I had worked in Ford's Theatre, wondered why the curtain was rung down so early; but, on going home, I would have been pretty sure to report a routine evening to the family. "They didn't finish 'Our American Cousin' tonight," I might have said. "Some trouble with the lights, I guess."

All this makes for a calm, well-ordered existence, with practically no nerve strain. Those men in derbies and I, provided we do not get hit by stray bullets, ought to live to a ripe old age if we take any kind of care of our kidneys at all. Dynasties may fall, cities may collapse, and the world be brought down about our ears,

And I shall probably be wearing a derby

but, unless something hits us squarely in the back, we are sitting pretty.

I do rather dread the day, however, when I look at a photograph of the focal point of the World Revolution and see myself smirking into the camera with my back to the fighting. And the worst of it will be that I shall probably be wearing a derby.

Tell-Tale
Clues

UNLESS you are very smart and remember all that was taught you in school about how to cover up your tracks after you have committed a crime, you are going to be surprised at some of the things that I am about to write down for you. And I, in turn, shall be surprised if you read them. The average criminal has no idea how careful he has to be in order to keep on being a criminal and not just an ex-. He may think that he is being careful while he is at work, wearing silk gloves and walking on his ankles and all that, but unless he spends as much time looking around for tell-tale bits of evidence after he commits the crime as he spent in committing it, then he is leaving himself open for a terrible panning by *some*one, even if it is only the Chief of Police.

For example, on April 7, 1904, the vault in the Lazybones National Bank and Fiduciary Trust Co. of Illville, Illinois, was blown off, and if there had been anything in there worth taking away, it could easily have been done. As it was, the vault contained nothing but a hundred shares of Goldman Sachs, and the robbers, instead of taking these, added two hundred more shares of their own and made their get-away, leaving the bank stuck with three hundred shares instead of one hundred.

Attracted by the oaths of the safe-crackers as they walked down the street, the police rushed first to the Farmers' and Drovers' Bank, then to the First Congregational Church, and then to the Lazybones National where the explosion had taken place. They found that not only had the front been blown off the vault but the handle to the front door of the bank building was gone. It had evidently been pulled off in pique by one of the robbers when he found that the door would not open as easily as he thought it ought to.

After a thorough investigation of the premises, Captain Louis Mildew of the detective force turned to his aid and said, "If we can find the man who has this door knob in his hand, we shall have the man who cracked the safe." A week later a man was picked up in Zanesville who was carrying a door knob which corresponded in every detail with the one missing from the bank building. In spite of the fact that he claimed that it belonged to him and that he

They added two hundred more shares of their own

was carrying it to ward off rheumatism, he was arrested and later confessed.

Another case where carelessness on the part of the criminal led to his ultimate arrest and embarrassment is found on the records of police in Right Knee, New Jersey. A puddle-worker had been killed in a fight and his assailant had escaped, evidently several days before the crime was discovered (in fact, the evidence pointed to the killer having escaped several days before the murder, which didn't make sense). On looking over the ground where the body was found, the police discovered a man's wooden leg firmly gripped in the teeth of the dead man.

The name of the makers of the wooden leg, the Peter Pan Novelty Co., was also broadcast.

On the fourth day of the search a policeman saw a one-legged man sitting at a bar and, approaching him in a businesslike manner, said, "I represent the Peter Pan Novelty Co. and there is a payment due on an artificial limb bought from us last year. Could you see your way clear to giving us something at this time?"

The one-legged man immediately bridled and said hotly, "I pay you no more on that leg. It came off when I needed it most, and I haven't even been able to find it since. If you wish, I will put this in the form of a letter of complaint to the company."

"You can put it in the form of testimony before a judge, buddy," said the policeman, turning back his lapel where he had forgotten to pin his badge. "Come along with me."

And so, simply through careless haste in getting away without looking about for incriminating evidence, the man was caught, and had a pretty tough time convincing the jury that he had done the killing in self-defense and to save his sister's honor. It was later found that not only did he have no sister but that she had no honor.

Perhaps the most famous instance of carelessness was the discovery of the abductor of the Sacred White Elephant of Mistick, California. This was an inside job, for the elephant had been confined in a hut which was several sizes too small for her, making it impossible for anyone to enter from the outside. This much was certain.

The elephant, when it was first discovered in Mistick, had been neither white nor sacred, but was a camp follower of a circus, who had liked the town and stayed behind when the rest moved on. So the town whitewashed her and spread the report about that she was sacred, and used to charge two bits to take a walk around her, once around one way and back around the other.

The man who had turned the trick was a very wily elephant thief who had been in the business a long time but had never worked in white elephants before. He made all provisions for a quick get-away and, before the loss was discovered, had the prize out of town and well on its way down the coast. What he had neglected to do, however, was to brush off the sleeve of his coat, not realizing that, when frightened, a white elephant gives off a fine dusty powder which settles on the nearest objects and marks them as having been near a white elephant. And so it was that, as the crook was walking along a country road leading his ill-gotten gain, he was accosted by a local constable. Stopping Potts (the thief's name was Potts), he said, "What's that white dust on your coat shoulder?"

"I just left my girl," said Potts.

"Does your girl wear white elephant powder?" asked the constable, very comical. "That's white elephant powder and it's off that elephant."

"What elephant?" said Potts in surprise, looking behind him. "Oh, *that* elephant?"

The thief tried to escape by hiding behind the beast; but the constable could see his legs and feet from the other side and placed him under arrest.

So you will see that it is the little things that count in successful police evasion, and the sooner our criminals realize this the fewer humiliating arrests there will be.

The Calf
in the Closet

FOR a man who is very fond of animals, I find myself oppressed by a strange phobia. I am afraid to go into my clothes-closet because there is a two-headed calf in there. Perhaps this needs a little explanation.

Several weeks ago I mentioned a birthday which was in the offing. It arrived, exactly on schedule, and with it several mementoes from loving friends, among them a two-headed calf. Perhaps this still needs a little explanation. I don't seem to be able to make it sound plausible.

On the morning of my birthday I was called on the telephone by a friend who asked me if I knew anything about getting people out of jail. The call was from the jail itself, and it transpired that two of my buddies were incarcerated there, and that I was indirectly the cause.

The day before, in passing a second-hand shop, they had seen a stuffed, two-headed calf among the chipped busts of Sir Walter Scott and suits of armor, and had decided that it

267

was the very thing for a *cadeau* for old Bob on his birthday. The man in the store assured them that I was a very lucky fellow to be getting it, as he had had several calls to rent it out at three dollars a night. And, besides, it was a very attractive property in itself.

It being not a very large calf (about the size of a sheep-dog without foliage), they took it with them in their automobile, giving it a place of honor in the rumble seat. From then on their trail is a little obscured, but they took the gift about quite a bit, showing it off to various friends, doubtless amid good-natured laughter at my expense.

On their way home that night they found themselves (or rather, were found by a policeman) exceeding one of the more absurd speed limits in a suburban community, and were ordered to draw up to the curb. The officer, in that hail-fellow-well-met manner of traffic policemen, started searching the car for liquor.

He found no liquor, but he did find a two-headed calf, which confused him even more than a case of rye would have done. There being no specific charge of "driving an automobile with a two-headed calf," he arrested them on the more conventional charge of "drunken driving." When there is a two-headed calf in the rumble seat, it seems hardly necessary to look for liquor. They were not even given the benefit of a sobriety test. The cop was no fool.

So, on presenting myself at the station-house with my pockets full of gold pieces, I not only had the satisfaction of seeing my friends set free, but also of receiving the custody of the calf, with their blessings.

I took it with me into my automobile (that calf got a lot of riding, what with one thing and another) and took it home with me. Even then I wasn't really crazy about it, although I could see that it must have been cute when it was in the pink. But somehow a stuffed animal is not really the same sort of pal that a live one is.

Not having any precedent for bedding-down two-headed calves, I put my new-found treasure into my clothes-closet—rather quickly, I am afraid. I turned its heads towards the wall, as there was a look about the four eyes that I did not like to think of as piercing the closet door in my direction when I was in bed. And then I shut the door and tried to forget.

But forgetting has not been easy. If I had left the thing out in the room where I could see it, I might have got up courage enough to take it out some day and get that three dollars rental on it. But not being able to see it, yet knowing that it is in that closet, so quiet and static, with its tail turned toward me, has gradually got on my nerves. I have a feeling that it has turned around by now and is waiting, heads on, for me to open the door. And I cannot

I circle even the vicinity of the closet

bring myself even to take a peek. A peek would be even worse than a bold sally into the closet.

I have now worn the same suit for nine days, and with the cool weather coming on, I am going to need a change pretty soon. But, with the passing of each day, the terror grows stronger, and I have now reached the point where I circle even the vicinity of the closet on my way in and out of the room. It is definitely beyond my powers to open that door, and what is more, I don't want to be anywhere near when some one else opens it.

I, who a short time ago, even doubted the existence of such a thing as a two-headed calf, am now reduced to a craven Frankenstein by the very proximity of one. (I didn't really create the monster—that took a trickier hand than mine—but I did bail it out of jail.)

So, anyone who feels the need of a stuffed two-headed calf may have one by calling at my room some day when I am out and opening the first closet door to the left. And even with the calf gone I shall never feel the same about that closet again.

More
Fauna

THIS seems to be the open season for
gerbers and zaylies. Everywhere strange
things are popping out of the sea and land,
wagging their heads and tails at people, and
then ducking back again. This sort of thing
takes a man's mind off his work.

The sea-serpent of Loch Ness has had a lot
of publicity, and I have already called your
attention to the What-Is-It which was caught
off Tampa, Florida, with legs like a child's in a
bunny-suit and a face like the Invisible Man's.
And now comes "The Mystery Animal of the
Tennessee Hills." What did someone do—
leave the gate to Hell open?

The Mystery Animal of the Tennessee Hills
looks, according to reports, like a giant kangaroo and is "fast as lightning." It runs and
leaps across fields, devouring your police dogs,
leaving nothing but their head and shoulders,
and, in general, behaving in a perfectly rotten
manner toward the livestock and citizenry of
South Pittsburgh, Tennessee.

The worst part of all this business is that there really is no good reason why there shouldn't be such animals. Why should there be a hippopotamus? If you had never seen a hippopotamus before, would you believe it? Would you *want* to believe it? Wouldn't you say "Bosh!" if someone told you about it?

I see no reason why we should take the scoffings of scientists seriously. They don't even take each other seriously. There is probably no more gullible group in the world than the scientists of today, according to the scientists of tomorrow. So let's not take any back talk out of them about gerbers and zaylies.

We accept hippopotami because there are a lot of them around (too many, if you ask me), but why couldn't there be an animal that has had the decency to keep under cover for a couple of thousand years but which, now in its present generation, has developed a youngster with some spirit that wants to see the world?

Dr. William Beebe, who spends a lot of time under water, says that the Loch Ness "sea-serpent" is, in his opinion, nothing but a giant squid. What does he mean "nothing but"? I don't care whether it is a squid or a gerber: as long as it is giant, I don't want it following me about.

"Just a giant octopus"; "just a giant beaver" —what good does it do to know that family name, if the thing itself looks awful? I think a giant beaver would be much worse than a medium-sized zaylie, even if the zaylie were twice as big as the giant beaver. I wouldn't even want to meet a giant rabbit.

It makes no difference whether you call them by the name of some well-known species or call them "deemies." That thing in the Tennessee hills may be the offspring of a kangaroo escaped from a circus and some attractive domestic animal it happened to meet in the woods, or it may be something that has been saving up ever since prehistoric days to take just one whirl in 1934 around South Pittsburgh, Tennessee. The fact remains that it frightens people just to look at it, and that's enough. Who are we to say that it doesn't exist?

I wish that you could take just one look at that photograph of the Thing they caught off Tampa, Florida.

Down
with Pigeons

S T. FRANCIS of Assisi (unless I am getting him mixed up with St. Simeon Stylites, which might be very easy to do as both their names begin with "St.") was very fond of birds, and often had his picture taken with them sitting on his shoulders and pecking at his wrists. That was all right, if St. Francis liked it. We all have our likes and dislikes, and I have more of a feeling for dogs. However, I am not *against* birds as a class. I am just against pigeons.

I do not consider pigeons birds, in the first place. They are more in the nature of people; people who mooch. Probably my feeling about pigeons arises from the fact that all my life I have lived in rooms where pigeons came rumbling in and out of my window. I myself must have a certain morbid fascination for pigeons, because they follow me about so much—and with evident ill will. I am firmly convinced that they are trying to haunt me.

Although I live in the middle of a very large city (well, to show you how large it is—it is the largest in the world) I am awakened every morning by a low gargling sound which turns out to be the result of one, or two, or three pigeons walking in at my window and sneering at me. Granted that I am a fit subject for sneering as I lie there, possibly with one shoe on or

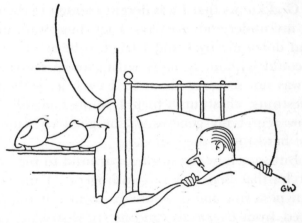

Pigeons walking in at my window and sneering at me

an unattractive expression on my face, but there is something more than just a passing criticism in these birds making remarks about me. They have some ugly scheme on foot against me, and I know it. Sooner or later it will come out, and then I can sue.

This thing has been going on ever since I was in college. In our college everybody was

276

very proud of the pigeons. Anyone walking across the Yard (Campus to you, please) was beset by large birds who insisted on climbing up his waistcoat and looking about in his wallet for nuts or raisins or whatever it is you feed pigeons (bichloride would be my suggestion, but let it pass).

God knows that I was decent enough to them in my undergraduate days. I let them walk up and down my back and I tried to be as nice as I could without actually letting them see that I was not so crazy about it. I even gave them chestnuts, chestnuts which I wanted myself. I now regret my generosity, for good chestnuts are hard to get these days.

But somehow the word got around in pigeon circles that Benchley was antipigeon. They began pestering me. I would go to bed at night, tired from overstudy, and at six thirty in the morning the Big Parade would begin. The line of march was as follows: Light on Benchley's window sill, march once in through the open window, going "Grumble-grumble-grumble" in a sinister tone. Then out and stand on the sill, urging other pigeons to come in and take a crack at it.

There is very little fun in waking up with a headache and hearing an ominous murmuring

I tried to be as nice as I could

noise, with just the suggestion of a passing shadow moving across your window sill. No man should be asked to submit to this *all* his life.

I once went to Venice (Italy), and there, with the rest of the tourists, stood in awe in the center of St. Mark's Piazza, gazing at the stately portals of the church and at the lovely green drinks served at Florian's for those who don't want to look at the church all of the time.

It is an age-old custom for tourists to feed corn to the pigeons and then for the pigeons to crawl all over the tourists. This has been going on without interruption ever since Americans discovered Venice. So far as the records show, no pigeon has ever failed a tourist—and no tourist has ever failed a pigeon. It is a very pretty relationship.

In my case, however, it was different. In the first place, the St. Mark's pigeons, having received word from the American chapter of their lodge, began flying at me in such numbers and with such force as actually to endanger my life. They came in great droves, all flying low and hard, just barely skimming my hat and whirring in an ugly fashion with some idea of intimidating me. But by that time I was not to be intimidated, and, although I ducked very low and lost my hat several times, I did not give in. I even bought some corn from one of the vendors and held it out in my hand, albeit with bad grace. But, for the first time in centuries, no pigeon fell for the corn gag. I stood alone in the middle of St. Mark's Square, holding out my hand dripping with kernels of golden corn, and was openly and deliberately snubbed. One or two of the creatures walked up to within about ten feet of me and gave me a nasty look, but not one gave my corn a tumble. So I decided the hell with them and ate the corn myself.

Now this sort of thing must be the result of a very definite boycott, or, in its more aggressive stage, an anti-Benchley campaign. Left to myself, I would have only the very friendliest feelings for pigeons (it is too late now, but I might once have been won over). But having been put on my mettle, there is nothing that I can do now but fight back. Whatever I may be, I am not yellow.

Here is my plan. I know that I am alone in this fight, for most people like pigeons, or, at any rate, are not antagonized by them. But single-handed I will take up the cudgels, and I hope that, when they grow up, my boys will carry on the battle on every cornice and every campus in the land.

Whenever I meet a pigeon, whether it be on

my own window sill or walking across a public park, I will stop still and place my hands on my hips and wait. If the pigeon wants to make the first move and attack me, I will definitely strike back, even to the extent of hitting it with my open palm and knocking it senseless (not a very difficult feat, I should think, as they seem to have very little sense).

If they prefer to fight it out by innuendo and sneering, I will fight it out by innuendo and sneering. I have worked up a noise which I can make in my throat which is just as unpleasant sounding as theirs. I will even take advantage of my God-given power of speech and will say: "Well, what do you want to make of it, you waddling, cooing so-and-sos?" I will glare at them just as they glare at me, and if they come within reach of my foot, so help me, St. Francis, I will kick at them. *And* the next pigeon that strolls in across my window ledge when I am just awakening, I will catch with an especially prepared trap and will drag into my room, there to punch the living daylights out of him.

I know that this sounds very cruel and very much as if I were an animal hater. As a matter of fact, I am such a friend of animals in general that I am practically penniless. I have been known to take in dogs who were obviously im-

postors and put them through college. I am a
sucker for kittens, even though I know that one
day they will grow into cats who will betray and
traduce me. I have even been known to pat a

*I have worked up a noise which . . . is just as
unpleasant sounding as theirs*

tiger cub, which accounts for my writing this
article with my left hand.

But as far as pigeons go, I am through. It is
a war to the death, and I have a horrible feeling that the pigeons are going to win.

Love
in Hollywood

THE seeming prevalence of divorce in Hollywood may be explained away by the fact that Hollywood divorces rate more publicity than any others, and so just seem more prevalent. But this does not explain why people in the movie colony can't get engaged, married or divorced without putting on a routine. You would think that they were smuggling opium into the country, the way they duck back and forth.

Nobody in Hollywood ever just goes and gets married, the way people do in other parts of the country. They never even get engaged. It takes at least six months for the male to circle around the female and dart away again, like polyps or Japanese sand-fish. It must be the climate.

Let us say that Norman LeRoy and Maida Marston work together in a picture and, what with the heat of the lights and the necessity for re-takes, find that they are in love with each other. There certainly is no harm in that. Well,

283

there is harm in it, but it's done all over the world, and with much more directness. Joe Doaks and Meridian Blevitch, of Utica, N. Y., fall in love, too.

As is customary under such circumstances, Norman LeRoy and Maida Marston see a lot of each other at the Cocoanut Grove and other public places; for, after all, that's the whole idea of liking someone, isn't it? They are seen dancing together, eating together and, if you happen out on the porch suddenly, necking together. This, my spies tell me, is only what goes on everywhere.

But, when confronted with the evidence, Miss Marston says: "I like Norman very much, but we are just good friends." And Norman says: "I never heard of Miss Marston, except professionally." This goes on for a few weeks, and they become engaged to be married.

Now, becoming engaged to be married has, with the broadening of our standards, been accepted as quite *au fait*. It is even the conventional thing to do. But Mr. LeRoy and Miss Marston shun the reputation for it as they would the reputation of being lepers. When discovered at Palm Beach together, Miss Marston says: "Of course, I am very fond of Mr. LeRoy, but we are just good friends." And Mr.

284

LeRoy says: "Who? Miss Marston? Never heard of her—except, of course, professionally."

Eventually, as so often happens in cases of engagement, they get married. A mistake, perhaps, but who can cast even the second stone?

"Miss Marston? Never heard of her—except, of course, professionally"

So, when they are man and wife, Mr. LeRoy takes up his legal residence at the Hollywood Athletic Club and Miss Marston goes to her mother's. And, when confronted with the City Clerk's ledger and the minister's day-book, Mr. LeRoy says: "I am flying today to New York, where I am taking up·sword-fishing. I have only the best wishes for Miss Marston, of whom I have never heard." And Miss Marston says: "Business calls me today to New Rochelle, N. Y. I am flying, but I had no idea that Mr. LeRoy was going to be on the same plane. We are just good friends."

They are such good friends that, in their own good time, they have a baby. This is a rather difficult spot. "I do know Miss Marston," admits Mr. LeRoy, "and I have a great admiration for her work."

And Miss Marston, holding the baby up to the camera so as to get a long-shot of the baby and a close-up of herself, says: "I am terribly fond of Norman, but there is nothing in this talk of our engagement. We are just good friends."

And the first that we really hear of the marriage is when they are divorced. Perhaps this is why Hollywood divorces get so much publicity. It's the first time the couple has broken down and admitted being married.